ABIGAIL NORFLEET JAMES, PHD

THE PARENTS' GUIDE TO

BOYS

HELP YOUR SON GET *the*
MOST OUT *of* SCHOOL *and* LIFE

LIVE OAK
BOOK COMPANY

Published by Live Oak Book Company
Austin, TX
www.liveoakbookcompany.com

Distributed by Live Oak Book Company

For ordering information or special discounts for bulk purchases, please contact Live Oak Book Company at PO Box 91869, Austin, TX 78709, 512.891.6100.

Design and composition by Greenleaf Book Group LLC
Cover design by Greenleaf Book Group LLC

Publisher's Cataloging-In-Publication Data
(Prepared by The Donohue Group, Inc.)
James, Abigail Norfleet.
    The parents' guide to boys : help your son get the most out of school and life / Abigail Norfleet James.—1st ed.
        p. ; cm.
    Includes index.
    Issued also as an ebook.
    1. Boys—Education. 2. Parenting. 3. Academic achievement. I. Title. II. Title: Parents guide to boys III. Title: Boys
LC1390 .J362 2013
371.8211   2012951972

ISBN: 978-1-936909-58-2
eBook ISBN: 978-1-936909-59-9

First Edition

CONTENTS

For John
Who helped me learn how to parent a boy
and
For Brennan
Who let us try

PREFACE

One of the most memorable songs from the 1954 Broadway version of *Peter Pan* is "I Won't Grow Up!" sung by Peter, accompanied by the Lost Boys singing the chorus. What's fascinating to note is that what Peter dreads most about growing up is *going to school*, which he equates with learning "to be a parrot" that merely recites "a silly rule." Even then school was considered a place where no right-thinking boy would be caught dead. After all, school was just about memorizing facts and not having the chance to do physically risky things.

Can't say as I blame Peter. I myself found school—especially the elementary grades—to be somewhat boring. I would much rather have been outdoors building forts or investigating the creek that ran beside our house. Even though I am female, I am fond of saying that I have the brain of a 14-year-old boy, with better verbal skills.

True, I spent a good deal of my childhood reading, but my favorite place to read was up in a tree. I lived in the country and had a lot of freedom to roam. My best friend lived within walking distance, and she and I spent a good part of our days outside.

We all went to school because it was required, but there was little pressure to succeed. Our parents just expected us to try our hardest at anything we did and they would be pleased. If you didn't do well in fourth grade, for example, the belief was that you would come along eventually. Either that or you would find something to do that didn't require academic success. My parents were teachers, and I can remember them talking about some student at their school who wasn't doing very well. They both agreed that he was probably going to do just fine running his family business, for which he already had an aptitude. Only students who really liked studying were expected to care about doing well and to worry about where they would go after high school.

Today, however, the stakes to succeed in school are huge. If you don't do well academically, the assumption is that you are going to fail at life. Everyone is expected to go to college or at least have some tertiary schooling. I've had fourth graders tell me they are worried they are not going to college because they can't pass their state academic standards tests, and without college, they don't know what they are going to do. Obviously they are parroting what they hear from the adults around them, but why should a 9-year-old child already be worried about what he is going to do when he is 19 or even 29? You probably have forgotten some of the interests you had in elementary school, or at least they have changed since then. And you probably have acquired skills you had no clue earlier in life that you would be good at, so you now have options you never knew were available when you were young.

If higher education shouldn't be expected of everyone, do we, as a society, want to go back to the early days of this country when only the very wealthy sent their children to school and most other children learned a trade? At that time, formal schooling and learning a trade were generally offered only to boys. Now, however, education seems to favor girls; in fact, almost 60% of the students who graduate from colleges and universities in the United States are women. But must a person have an academic background to get ahead in life? Can people no longer earn a good living based on skills acquired either on the job or in directed training? If those two beliefs are true, then many boys are in serious trouble.

I grew up at the boys' school where my parents taught and then I attended a girls' high school. It never occurred to me, living in either single-gender environment, that anything we did was limited to one sex or the other. There were no labels of appropriate or inappropriate interests or activities because of gender. If you were not good at something it was not because you were female; it was because you were not good at it. No one ever said to me that math was something girls were not supposed to be interested in. True, there weren't a lot of girls at my school who were interested in math, but the fact that I was didn't make me less of a girl. My son was raised at the boys' school where I grew up because I was teaching there then. He became interested in singing classical music partially because he had seen the big boys in the school choir singing that music.

When students enter an all-boys' school, they usually come with stereotypical attitudes about favorite subjects and abilities. They will change those assumptions when they see the school quarterback singing lead in the winter musical, even though they realize he is wearing makeup (it helps that he gets to kiss the girl!). Boys who have decided they don't like to read change their minds when they are given books that appeal to them. In his coed elementary school, my son once had to read a book entitled *The Hundred Dresses*. It's an excellent book with a great lesson about bullying, but it's better suited to girls than to boys. On the other hand, many boys' schools include *Pride and Prejudice* on their reading list. If the study of this work focuses on Elizabeth Bennett, boys aren't usually very interested, but shift the focus to Mr. Darcy, they will read the story and become fascinated by what it meant to be a man in Regency England.

I left teaching to attend graduate school and find out what was known about how boys learn. Mostly what I discovered was that boys were much more likely to be identified with learning disabilities than were girls. It didn't make a lot of sense to me that simply being male put children at academic risk, but then I realized that girls were being used as the standard of what good students looked like.

Did that mean that boys couldn't learn? I knew that wasn't true because I'd taught boys successfully for years. Besides, most men are pretty successful as adults, so that must mean the ways boys learned were different. Also, because I had taught girls in girls' schools I knew that the approaches I used with boys were not the same as the approaches I used with girls. Consequently, I wrote a book for teachers—*Teaching the Male Brain: How Boys Think, Feel & Learn in School*—about how boys learn. Since then, I've been invited to visit boys' schools to talk with the teachers about pedagogical approaches to use with their students. When I am there, I am frequently asked to talk to the parents as well because I am the mother of a boy.

This book is the result of lots of requests from parents and teachers alike to present the information from my first book in ways that would help mothers and fathers of boys prepare their sons for school.

I didn't know all of the ideas and realities discussed in this book as I was raising my son. Many of these lessons were learned on the job, and I didn't get the point until after the fact. As parents, you and I are doing the best we can, and I hope these suggestions will help you navigate the stormy seas of raising a boy in this 21st-century world. I continue to learn about boys because I'm always talking to teachers and parents about the boys they work with. If you have a comment or a question, feel free to contact me through my website: www.abigailnorfleetjames.com.

ACKNOWLEDGMENTS

══════

Every book is the creation of a group of people, and the author is simply the person who took the time to write. The people who have assisted me with this are many and varied.

The genesis of this book is the parents whose sons attend boys' schools around the world where I have spoken. When I go to the boys' schools, I always offer to speak to the parents since I am both a teacher of boys and the parent of a boy. Over and over, the parents have asked me to put into writing some of the suggestions for helping their boys do better in school, and so I have. Also, the teachers at these schools have indicated that their job would be a bit easier if there were a source they could provide for the parents.

The schools of the International Boys School Coalition and the member schools of the National Association of Single-Sex Public Education have been very generous in inviting me in and sharing their secrets of successful education of boys. Brad Adams, the executive director of the ISBC has been a supporter and friend and I am very grateful for his encouragement and help in all that I do.

I had been a teacher for years before I became a mother and so I was struck by the differences in dealing with children from opposite sides of the desk, so to speak. From the beginning, I depended on my husband to let me know what worked with boys; after all, he had been a boy, I had not, even though I had grown up around a lot of boys. Many of these suggestions came from him. Our son was a unique person from the start who challenged all of my ideas about how to parent. We were determined that he should find his own way in the world, and he has. His trip has not been without difficulties, but he is in charge of himself and we are proud of what he has done in his life. Both my husband and I have been late bloomers, and our son seems headed in that direction as well. That tends to result in some parental concern, but we know we gave him a good foundation.

Friends are the best resources there are. Lori Howard leads this group. We met in graduate school, and besides just being a good friend I can giggle with, her wise counsel has helped me more than I can say. Some friends have been a great source of help by serving as a sounding board for ideas and providing new insights into solutions. Other friends are good parents who have served as great role models. My brother and sister-in-law and my husband's siblings and spouses have been some of the best examples, as was my cousin Dick Joyner. Denny and Dana Macklin have raised three fine sons who are equally fine fathers. I am proud to know them. Ann Snider is the model for the mother who is dealing with her son's issues by working with him for solutions. She introduced me to Casey Quinlan and Bart Levy, who have helped me with my website and have reformatted the information in this book so that it is aimed for parents and not for teachers. They have helped me get my message across to a wider world.

When I wrote my books for teachers, finding a publisher was not difficult because I was a teacher writing for teachers. Finding a publisher for this work was more difficult because there are lots of parental-help books. When I did find Greenleaf Book Group, the first person to work with me was Hobbs Allison, who it turns out is a graduate of Hampden-Sydney College in Virginia, one of the very few all male colleges in the United States. He understood what I was trying to do and has been a valued supporter. Linda O'Doughda pushed me to make this understandable and readable and has turned into a friend as well. I have come to value her insights and input.

Please remember, this work is based on personal experiences that may not work for you or for your child. The suggestions are also aimed at the average child, and most children vary from the average to some extent or another. You will find that some of the strategies will work with your son and some will not. I've tried to cover all the bases, but the most important thing I've learned from watching good parents is that they are consistent and caring.

INTRODUCTION

In May 2011, Mike Rowe, the host of Discovery Channel's show
Dirty Jobs, testified before the United States Senate Committee on
Commerce, Science, and Technology. Rowe's remarks centered on
the lack of individuals who were being trained to do the "dirty jobs"
featured on his show. He cited several instances where all the people
in a particular job were over 50 years old; he also mentioned that
some job opportunities went unfilled because there were no people
who were trained to do these essential functions. These remarks
came during a time with one of the highest unemployment rates
in memory. Rowe finished his remarks by urging the committee
to encourage the development of training programs because
"closing the skills gap doesn't just benefit future tradesmen and
the companies desperate to hire them. It benefits people like me,
and anyone else who shares my addiction to paved roads, reliable

bridges, heating, air-conditioning, and indoor plumbing. The skills gap is a reflection of what we value. To close the gap, we need to change the way the country feels about work."

Most of the individuals who would fill these skilled positions are male. The concern is that boys are being pushed into academic tracks in school both by parents and by a society that views this as the way to a more economically robust future. This trend is based on a belief that trades are not going to provide the upwardly mobile life that society says we all want. No matter that the boy is not interested in academics, that he likes putting things together and taking them apart, and that there is a crying need for skilled workers. He has got to go to college first.

Yes, this book is full of suggestions for parents eager to make sure that their sons do well in school. The assumption is that all parents want their sons to go to college, complete some graduate program, and become a success. My father told me that if you love what you do, it isn't work. The flip side is that no matter how much money you make, if you don't like what you do, it is torture. What parents really want is for their sons to be happy and successful in whatever they do. Children are likely to be a bit more successful if they can read, write, and do math well. Those skills are learned early in school. So even if you know your son is likely to be a welder, a plumber, an electrician, a banker, or a lawyer, helping him do well in school at the beginning will help him in the end.

But school is not only about academics. You will find that

helping your son succeed in school has more to do with his personal attributes than with the arithmetic he is learning. What he needs for you to teach him is that failure is the first step toward success; that insisting on getting your own way usually makes other people unhappy or mad; and that intrinsic motivation lasts whereas extrinsic motivation, like money, is temporary.

Do not be tempted to be your son's academic teacher! You are his life teacher. If he can't do his homework, your job is to help him figure out what he doesn't know so he can ask his classroom teacher for help the next day. Please, do not do his work for him. This is very difficult, I know. I found myself saying to my son, "Let me show you how to do that" and taking hold of the pencil. That is the key: keep your hands off of his work. Even if you are giving him directions, he must do the actual work. Yes, it will be messy. That is a matter for his teacher to deal with. You may be surprised to see that his handwriting is not as messy as others in his class and that he is making progress.

You will hear me say this—you are not to do your son's work for him—over and again, and the reason is because boys are pragmatists. If they can get someone else to do their work, *they will*. Remember Tom Sawyer? He was pretty skilled at getting other people to paint the fence for him. Also, by doing his work, you send the message to your son that you don't think he is capable of doing the work. That is not a lesson you want him to get from you.

Another point is that he is to be responsible for getting his work to and from school. The day will come when you find out that he never turned in his work because he left the directions at school, left the completed work at home, or couldn't find it in his backpack in class. This is *not your problem*; it is his. You can ask him what you can do to help, but your help should not involve your handling any of the paper involved and it should not involve a dash to school with the forgotten paperwork. You can help him by showing him what you do to be organized and keep track of all that you are responsible for.

Be forewarned: To get you to do his work for him, your son may tell you that his teacher doesn't explain things well, or that the teacher doesn't like him or doesn't like boys. Some teachers are good at working with boys and others don't seem to appreciate their energy and senses of humor. Learning to work for someone whose style doesn't fit yours is one of the best lessons we all learn in school. Boys find that lesson particularly hard for many reasons. In fact, the point of this book is to give you some insights into why your son approaches life the way he does and what you can do to help him in school and out.

What Follows

At the moment, there's a dispute among the experts as to whether or not the variations in behavior that we see in boys and girls are due to differences in brain development or to societal expectations of men and women or to a combination of both effects. The first chapter will introduce you to the general points in this "nature vs. nurture" controversy. True, this debate has been going on for many years, but the information in this chapter will give you a brief background in what we know at the moment and how you can integrate both approaches into dealing with your son.

Chapters 2 through 6 are divided into various age/academic levels: Infants and Toddlers, Preschool and Kindergarten, Elementary School, Middle School, and High School. (After all, this is a book written by a teacher to help parents prepare their sons for school.) Each chapter starts with information about the changes in the brain and the body that are typical for a child of that age.

If your son is very little, you will certainly find the early chapters to be of interest, but the later chapters will help you see why what you are doing now will help you and your son later. If your son is older, reading the earlier chapters will help you understand how your son got to be the way he is and will give you some suggestions on how to mend fences.

Depending on the age/stage, the chapter may then provide some information about skills or activities that are particularly well suited for a child at that level. For example, the chapter on elementary school includes a section on developing independence because it is as grade-schoolers that children first start to pull away from their families. The chapter on middle school will cover thoughts on electronics and virtual entertainment because boys at this age are most interested in these pastimes.

Much of the information in the childhood development area is supported by research, but not biologically based research. It is clear that most age-appropriate behavior is shaped by culture and by environment. That does not mean that gender is not involved— it is, absolutely—but this behavior varies from culture to culture among children of the same age, so you have some influence on change here.

Another section that will appear in each chapter is a description of activities you can engage in with your son that will help him be prepared for what he is going to face in school. For example, the first activity is to read to your son. Your job is not to teach your child to read; your job is to familiarize him with the language around him and to encourage him to enjoy reading. When children who have been read to at home get to school, they are simply better ready for reading instruction. You are going to find out that reading to your child provides many different benefits aside from language development, and it is the single most important thing you can do to help your child succeed in school.

Some of the other activities may surprise you, such as making sure that your child has chores appropriate to his age level and encouraging your son to join in the family discussions at mealtime. You should play games with your child, but those which suit his cognitive development. In this way, you will not be tempted to let him win. As your son grows up, there will be fewer and fewer activities he will be willing to let you do with him, but laying a good foundation early will mean that he will likely come home in high school for an occasional family game night, for example.

Each chapter also includes suggestions from this teacher about ways you can help your child navigate the requirements of education. As your son's parent, you will want to help him, but you are going to discover that too much help for boys will result in lack of effort on their part.

Because I've divided this book according to school levels, it is sometimes hard to see the whole boy and how the various stages of school affect his development. The process of moving out of toddlerhood and into childhood takes time. There will be setbacks, with three steps forward and one step back, until suddenly, it seems, your toddler is off on his own. Chapter 7 is designed to help you see that total process. For example, language development is a major issue for boys, but once they can read, your job isn't over. He needs for you to talk with him and continually help him understand the art of communication both in writing and talking.

Finally, the last section will list a number of resources and helps you may find useful. I've suggested books to help you explore further the "nature vs. nurture" debate if you wish; authors of books that boys have enjoyed; websites for sources to help you and your son as he begins to make decisions for his adult life; and a host of other information.

What I hope you get out of this book

Whether or not your son intends to go to college, being a good learner in primary and secondary school is an important start in life. This book offers you practical, doable suggestions for what you as a parent can do to help your child become a more effective student at every stage. Brian Jacques, the author of the *Redwall* series, which is very popular with boys, left school at age 15 and he then worked as a sailor and a truck driver. He didn't even graduate from high school and yet he wrote wonderful tales for children. Obviously, he learned good language skills early in his schooling.

What you want for your child is to become a confident, capable person. School is a huge part of the journey to get there; at the beginning, your son needs your help in the process. If you do your job right, your help will no longer be needed as he leaves school.

Please remember that the more you do for your son, the less he will do. It is your job to teach him to do his own work, to be responsible for his own belongings, and to pay attention to the effect he has on people around him. He won't learn those lessons if you do those tasks for him. "But he is so little," I hear you say, and "he doesn't do those jobs well." Of course; that is the point. He knows that if he only tries a bit, you will take over and then the job is done to your satisfaction. What you should want is the job done by him, no matter what the outcome is.

I promise, this isn't that hard, but it does require you to be consistent and to listen to him. If he is doing his work, then you are doing the right thing, no matter what other people tell you. Boys are so much fun, so enjoy your boy. He absolutely needs you to be there for him. The suggestions in the pages that follow will help.

CHAPTER 1

ARE BOYS DIFFERENT?

Of all the animals, the boy is the most unmanageable.

—Plato

This is not a book about parenting boys. This is a book about how to be the parent of a schoolboy. Plato recognized a long time ago that boys in an educational setting could be difficult, and that does not seem to have changed much in the intervening years. In fact, if you keep up with trends in education, you'll know that one of the major problems teachers are dealing with at the moment is boys. Specifically, they aren't doing as well as girls academically and socially and few people seem to know what to do about it. You will find disparate opinions on the subject ranging from those who are convinced the solution is boy-friendly single-gender schools to those who are just as sure that the only difference between boys and girls is socially constructed and so coed education is the answer. Neither extreme seems to meet all needs because children do not fall into two mutually exclusive groups; some girls are more like boys and some boys have the skills and interests of girls. What your boy requires to succeed is unique, and you, as his parent, must be there to support him and everyone else who is trying to help. He needs to trust you to be on his side, but he doesn't need you to make excuses for him.

Let's start by taking a look at what we do know about boys and girls before I get into more details about the current debate over the best way to educate boys.

Sex or Gender?

Sex refers to biology and gender refers to the way a person expresses his or her sexual identity. Sex is not a totally dichotomous term, however, as there are individuals who exist whose genes are not either XY (male) or XX (female). Their sex chromosomes might be unconventionally configured as XO (Turner's Syndrome), XXY (Klinefelter Syndrome), and XYY. Additionally, there are individuals who have conventional genetic configuration but whose physical expression of those genes is clearly ambiguous. These individuals may appear to be one sex when their genes are for the opposite sex and are considered to be "intersex." Without a genetic test, therefore, we can't be sure of someone's sex.

Gender, on the other hand, refers to how we feel about ourselves, and that can be even more confusing. Most adults will talk about the "male" and "female" sides of their personalities, admitting that they can and do have aspects of both. Throughout this book, I will always refer to gender because right from infancy there are so many environmental pressures on a child to behave in certain ways that it becomes difficult to separate out sex from gender.

The expression of gender is a serious issue for boys. The boys' schools I work with are very sure that part of the problem is that boys may not see a lot of men in their daily life. Girls see their mothers, female teachers, the lunch ladies in the cafeteria, and so forth. Many boys, however, live in houses without an adult male and, in elementary school, are unlikely to see male teachers. What it means to be male is a huge issue for these boys, one which you, as a parent, need to help your son face. Boys know they are male; they are just not always sure what it means to be male.

Are boys and girls different?

Boy or girl? is usually the first question asked when someone learns of a new baby. With the highly technical imaging tests available today, most parents find out the sex of their child before birth. But, what do we mean when we say a child is "all boy" or "typically girl?" Your child will probably be like the stereotypical male or female in some respects and not in others. Yes, I am well aware that every child is different, but most children are alike in many areas and that is why stereotypes exist.

The point is that individual children may or may not match the stereotypes. When you look at a lot of children together, you will see patterns of behavior that are considered typical for boys or girls. So when I talk about boy behavior and your son does not act that way, it does not mean I am wrong or your son is not a typical boy. It means your son's behavior is not stereotypical. A boy who is an early reader or who doesn't like competitive group sports may need a bit of help finding other children who share his interests, but they are certainly out there.

Children who don't fit the appropriate sexual stereotype can have trouble, but not necessarily. Girls who are tomboys usually have far fewer difficulties in life than do boys who are a bit feminine. What your son needs is your support in his interests. A boy who would rather take tap dancing at age six instead of playing in a soccer league will develop many of the same skills. Yes, he may get a bit of grief from his friends as they grow up because dancing is "for girls," but once those boys discover girls and find out that girls think a boy who can dance is really cool, they may come to the dancer for a few lessons. What your son needs is for you to support him in his interests, not to coerce him into doing things you think he should be interested in. A lot of my boy students admitted that they played sports because their fathers wanted them to play, not because they were interested in playing the game. Find out what your son wants to do and cheer him on, no matter what the activity. Kevin Clash, the muppeteer who makes Elmo come alive, was interested in puppetry when he was very little. He made his first puppet out of the lining of his father's raincoat. His mother's remark was that, in the future, before he cut up family clothes, he should ask for permission, but she didn't get mad. In fact, she encouraged him to present puppet shows to the neighborhood children. His parents have been totally supportive of him even though his interest was unusual, especially in the working-class section of Baltimore where he grew up. His parents' support was a huge factor in his career and he originally named Elmo's parents for his own.

Nature or Nurture?

The discussion of whether genetics or environment play a larger part in the development of our personality is a thorny one. No one actually knows which factor has the greater influence although most of us hold strong opinions on the subject. Some believe that children come into the world as "blank slates" and are the sum of all of their environmental influences. Others believe that children bring with them certain temperaments and abilities which are obvious early and influence how they respond to environmental factors. Most believe that there is a balance between both genetics and environment and that is the approach that I will use. Consequently, I will start with a discussion of what is known about biology and then introduce what we know about how upbringing shapes us all. You may find the explanation of the relative effects of genetics and environment somewhat extensive, but this subject is complex, and I want you to understand this: neither side can be sure that what they say is completely right. Yes, that includes me, and for this reason I will often say "most" or "many" rather than "all" children.

WHAT MAKES BOYS AND GIRLS DIFFERENT?

The real answer to the question "what makes boys and girls different?" is that we don't actually know. And to further complicate the matter, it is hard to measure whether they really are different. Yes, I know that your son is different from girls of the same age, but part of that is because you have raised him to be a boy. When he was a baby, he got trucks and balls for presents and he was dressed in blue jeans and baseball caps. He got a stuffed bear to cuddle, not a doll. We don't know if he likes trucks because boys like wheeled toys or because he got lots of them as presents. Some research shows that children prefer gender-specific toys and certainly the toy manufacturers believe that to be true. Color alone will alert you to the different types of toys available for girls and those for boys.

It is nearly impossible to raise a child in a gender-neutral environment, although a few families have tried. The number of such children is small, however, and their experiences cannot be guaranteed to be free of gendered influences. Consequently, scientists are limited in their use of information from those families to figure out which behaviors associated with boys are due to biology and which are due to the way the boys are raised. You may have seen a discussion of this issue in the press, with some experts confident that children exhibit gender-specific behavior strictly as a result of the way they are raised and others just as sure that it is all due to biology.

Part of the problem in trying to raise gender-neutral children is that the parents may inadvertently give their children the impression that gender-typical behavior is not correct. In these situations, the children will exhibit gender-neutral behavior because they want to please their parents, not because that is how they would like to react. I think the gendered behavior we see in children is due both to biology and environment. I know with certainty no one taught my son to make motor noises when he was playing with toy cars, but he did. On the other hand, he was very happy to wear a coat and tie when he dressed up because his father and all of the big boys at the school where I taught did so. He had learned that was gender appropriate attire for men.

Most of the research available on neuroscience and gender comes from scientists who look only at one portion of the brain or one set of behaviors. That makes it hard to know with any certainty if a particular part of the brain is responsible for a specific behavior or not. Another complication is that the technology involved in brain imaging is changing so fast the data from a brain study might not still be correct in a year or two. So why bother at all? Because much of the information validating gender differences is reasonably sure, and a growing body of research in education indicates that gender-specific educational approaches help both boys and girls.

I believe that boys and girls are different, but I'm also aware that a lot of what we see is based on differences in developmental rates and processes. For example, in late elementary school, due to the differences of the onset of puberty, most of the girls are taller than most of the boys. However, by the time they get to be 18-year-olds, most of the boys will be taller than the girls. Society says that boys should be taller than girls, and thus for little boys, it can be confusing to be the shortest kid in the class. The last child in a class to enter puberty is likely to be a boy, and by the time he hits his growth spurt, he may be very defensive about his lack of stature. Even though he grows rapidly through high school and overcomes the original height difference, he may still feel somewhat inadequate. His behavior is based on a difference that no longer exists, but habits die hard.

It is the educational information that interests me, particularly because boys have so much trouble in school. It doesn't seem fair that just being a boy would put a child at risk for academic failure, but the overwhelming number of children identified with learning issues and who are in academic jeopardy are boys. Because that is true all over the world, it would seem as if the issues that boys have in school are biologically based, or at the very least, their biology does not promote success in a traditional school environment.

EVIDENCE FOR BRAIN DIFFERENCES—NATURE

The differences in brain development between boys and girls are most obvious at birth and gradually diminish as children age. Whether or not those differences are the cause of the behavior that we associate with males and females is under a lot of scrutiny at the moment. Also, whether or not those differences disappear by adulthood is not agreed upon. For example, one of the most robust findings is that at birth, the left portion of the brain dedicated to language is developing a bit faster in girls than in boys. That has generally been cited as the reason why 20-month-old girls have twice the vocabulary of 20-month-old boys. Of course, some girls have small vocabularies and some boys use lots of words, but *on average*, this is true.

If adults are given a test in verbal intelligence, the results cannot be sorted by sex, and some researchers believe this is an indication that the differences in verbal skills have disappeared by the time individuals finish formal schooling. However, there is evidence that as adults, males and females do not process verbal information in the same way. Additionally, the tests for verbal skills have been designed in part to reduce gender differences. Even though the test results appear to indicate that there are no gender differences in verbal skills in adults, the evidence does not give a clear picture of the situation because the test is not designed to reveal any gender difference. A lot of the difficulty in sorting out whether or not gender differences exist has to do with the methods that are used to provide the evidence: assumptions are made about the underlying cause for the data, which is not good for scientific conclusions.

You will find that verbal skill development is a major topic in this book. The reason is two-fold: first, we know a lot about verbal development and what part of the brain is activated when we are engaged in using verbal skills; second, verbal skills are essential to school success. Research indicates that at least part of the problem for boys early in school is that they are slower than girls to develop verbal fluency. This means girls are more ready when they enter school to begin to learn to read than boys are. Even if you believe those who say that the differences start to disappear around the time children enter school (I'm not one of those, by the way), boys do not enter school with the same facility with language as girls do. It's been shown that even small differences create problems for boys early in school.

Some experts believe that the differences in the brain are too small to account for the differences in behavior that are observed. They propose that behavioral differences are actually caused by the way parents and others in the infant's environment react to the child. We don't know what effect differences in the brain have on behavior; nor do we know how much difference must exist to result in behavior attributed to neurological differences.

To say that the biological differences are too small to account for the behavioral differences is not supported by facts, only by supposition. Just believing something doesn't make it true. In fact, I believe that the biological differences are sufficient to support the notion that behavioral differences are due to brain differences, but I don't have any more facts at my disposal than do advocates for the other side. The difference is that the behavior I am referring to as gender specific tends to be seen in a wide variety of cultures as well as supported by data from primates. Culture does have an effect on the expression of behavior, but it would appear that the similar behaviors start with biology.

EVIDENCE FOR BRAIN CHANGES—NURTURE

As we grow and develop, our brain changes in response to our experiences. We know that as infants grow into children, their brains produce many connections, called dendrites, which expand the ability of the child to learn and to do all sorts of things. Then, as children grow and develop, the brain begins the process of removing dendrites that are not often used, which streamlines the brain's ability to function. The process called dendritic pruning enables us to simplify the thinking required to do repetitive tasks.

Think about the process of learning to drive a car. When you first got behind the wheel, it was all you could do to manage thinking about what you were doing with your feet and your hands at the same time to move the car forward. Then you had to pay attention to what was going on around the car so that you didn't run into other cars or a pedestrian. If someone was talking to you, you simply couldn't also pay attention to that as well. Over time, much of driving became a pattern of behavior that didn't require a lot of your attention. Now you can drive and do other things at the same time. (Not too many, please. You are less able to multitask than you think!) Dendritic pruning allows you to drive a car and do other things because the pathways for driving behavior have become routine and there aren't a lot of choices for you to make. When you are in heavy traffic or driving in bad weather, however, you find you need to pay close attention again because those situations require more than just the driving patterns you have established.

The experts who believe that the gender stereotypical behavior children exhibit is due to this sort of patterning assume that those behaviors exist because society expects boys and girls to behave in stereotypical ways. Children learn to behave in certain ways and then those patterns of behavior become set, just as your driving behavior is set. I would agree except that children with the same set of parents can behave in very different ways. For instance, I taught two brothers, one of whom was an athlete and the other—with a similar body type—was a computer nerd who never went outside.

Those who believe that gendered behavior is learned will explain such differences in siblings by saying the parents aren't being consistent in how they treat their children. The problem with this explanation is that we see similar patterns of behavior in children from very different families. For example, look at tomboys. Most of these girls don't like to wear dresses, prefer simple hairdos, and tend to be loud and rough in their play. If these girls come from widely differing families, why then is their behavior so similar, particularly when many of their parents actively try to suppress this behavior? It makes better sense to me that these girls share some biological predisposition to tomboy behavior rather than that they learned it from watching others or from their parents who wanted them to behave this way.

Does this mean your child may develop the way he does *in spite of* your efforts at parenting rather than *because of* those efforts? Well . . . yes. Don't panic. After all, think about yourself. You are not just the way your parents wanted you to be. At some point, you realized that you are not your parents and do not think exactly as they do. That is essentially what the angst of adolescence is all about: separating from your parents and becoming your own person. Remember that when your son gets to that stage so you will not grab him closer in an attempt to keep the little boy you can control. Much of his behavior he will have learned from you, but some of that behavior is simply part of who he is.

TWIN STUDIES

The standard method researchers use to assess how much of behavior is due to biology and how much is learned from the environment is to compare identical twins with fraternal twins. As you know, identical twins are genetically the same individual whereas fraternal twins are simply siblings born at the same time. True, fraternal twins are more alike than are conventional siblings so some of the measures are reflecting similar experiences. However, identical twins are more alike than any other members of the family, even when the twins are reared apart. And it is that last statement that is key. When identical twins are adopted into different families and have very different experiences, they are more like their twin than they are like anyone in their adoptive families, which reveals the important connection of genes with behavior. Even so, no individual is exactly like another, so we know that environment does have an effect.

Using twin studies, the belief is that human beings are somewhere between 50% and 70% determined by our biology. That is why we do need to discuss biology in describing how your son is growing up. More than half of him is due to his genetics, which came from his parents, after all. That makes teasing out the source of behavior even more complicated. Did he learn to rub his chin when he is puzzled because he watched you do it, or do you both share some genetic information that results in chin rubbing when you consider some problem? Many adoptees who have found their "birth parents" are astounded to see someone who walks as they do or has similar responses in certain situations. Clearly they couldn't have learned that behavior from their biological parent(s) because they weren't around that mother, father, or set of parents as they were growing up, so the behavior must be linked to genetic information in some way.

CONCLUSION

We know exactly what causes some behavior; reflexes are great examples. When the doctor hits your knee with a rubber hammer, your lower leg jerks out. The pathways for this effect are well known and everyone agrees on the causes. The point is everyone reacts to the hit on the knee in the same way—unless there is something wrong with a person's neurological system. The dilemma with psychology, as we've just seen, is that not everyone agrees on what causes the behaviors that are not due to reflexes.

Teachers deal with average children, and so I think it is worthwhile for those who work in education to understand what is true for the average child. Teachers, however, can come to expect all children to fit the mold of the average child and that can lead to problems. A boy who develops verbal skills early may be identified by a teacher as being exceptional when he is just a bit earlier to develop than his male peers. The parents of a boy who develops verbal skills a bit late may be led to believe that the delay is due to their lack of involvement in stimulating his verbal development when the boy may just be a bit slower to develop than others his age. On the other hand, the early reader may have had parents who read to him all the time and the later reader may come from a family where no one reads. It's frustrating, I know, but there's still so much scientists, medical professionals, and researchers just don't know.

However, because so many children *do have similar behaviors* even though they come from very different families, it makes sense that a lot of the behaviors we see are heavily influenced by brain development. That is why each of the chapters that follow will begin with what we know to be true about gender differences in changes in the brain at each level. But because changes in the brain cannot explain all of the gender differences we see, I've also included a discussion of the effects of environment as well. Sorry I can't be more definite than that, but at least you will get both sides of the issue.

CHAPTER 2

INFANTS AND TODDLERS

Boys are beyond the range of anybody's sure understanding, at least when they are between the ages of 18 months and 90 years.

—James Thurber

We can start the discussion in this chapter by asking the question: is the brain of a baby boy different from the brain of a baby girl? And the simple answer is, maybe. There is a tremendous amount of overlap in brain function and development, but in general scientists find consistent differences in a few areas. The differences are actually in structural development, not in specific brain structures. An expert looking at an MRI of an infant's brain cannot tell if the infant is male or female. But, if that expert looks at brain scans of a child every year or so, gender differences in the course of development are much more apparent. Probably no one completely fits the male brain or female brain pattern, but that doesn't mean we can't talk about differences.

People behave differently toward children based simply on what they believe to be the sex of the baby. Hand an adult an infant wrapped in a blue blanket and the adult will tell you how strong the little fellow is and how vigorously he moves. Hand another adult the same infant, wrapped in pink this time, and you will hear that the baby is sweet and delicate. When asked to describe their newborn children, parents frequently use sexually stereotypical adjectives to describe their children, adjectives that do not necessarily match descriptions given by other adults who do not know the sex of the children. We don't know whether having the nursery decorated in sex-specific colors will make a difference in infants, but because newborn babies see pastel colors as white, it probably won't scar a boy to put him in a pink blanket for the trip home from the hospital. However, he is going to be affected by the way he is treated by those around him.

What follows is information based on the latest research as of the time I am writing this.

Right Brain vs. Left Brain

You've heard the protests, haven't you? "I can't do math, I'm not left brained." "An artist has to be right brained." Sometimes people say such things to avoid subjects they don't like. But let's look deeper to see whether they really are limited by their brain.

The thinking part of our brains is composed of two similar but not identical hemispheres, which together are about the size of a cantaloupe. These hemispheres are surrounded by cerebrospinal fluid, which cushions the brain against blows to the head. Part of the left side of the brain appears to be programmed for language and part of the right for spatial skills. Of course, brains do much more than just those two tasks, but differences in those areas are apparent very early.

Research shows that at birth the left side of the brain is developing faster in girls and the right side is developing faster in boys. The left side of the brain is generally considered to be where the language center begins and the right side where spatial skills begin. These differences may explain why a 20-month-old girl has twice the vocabulary of a 20-month-old boy and why that same little boy can probably throw an object with more accuracy than the verbal little girl. Unfortunately, if you are not aware of that difference, a little boy can seem as if he is not as smart as the little girl because he doesn't talk very much. The commonly held belief is that verbal skills equal intelligence, and because of assumptions by adults around him, a nonverbal little boy will get the impression very early that he is not clever and not expected to excel in areas that require verbal skills.

The little boy's ability to throw a ball and hit the window is not usually seen as a mark of intelligence; in fact, it is viewed more often as an indication of how much trouble he is going to be later on. But the spatial skills that seem to be centered in the right hemisphere are very important in many academic areas, such as higher mathematics and physics, and in nonacademic areas, such as computer games. Certainly, some girls have good spatial skills, just as some boys have good verbal skills, but when children are very little, on average girls are better at verbal skills and boys better at spatial skills.

Two structures in the left hemisphere of the brain are involved in expressing language: one is responsible for the learning of words and the other is responsible for the production of language, including grammar. Both of these develop a bit faster in girls which may be the reason little boys have smaller vocabularies and have more trouble being able to string words together correctly when they begin to speak.

Adult males and females appear to have similar levels of verbal intelligence so the assumption is that while the male brain may start off with fewer sophisticated verbal skills, by adulthood those differences have evened out. However, new imaging techniques reveal that adult male and female brains don't process language in exactly the same way or in the same sections of the brain. Men and women perform in similar fashions on tests of verbal intelligence, which means that even though they are not doing the same thing in their brains with words, they have learned to produce similar products. In other words, school was successful. Culture assumes that males will always be behind females in verbal skills, and partially because school exaggerates shortcomings, boys may get the impression that their verbal skills will never be the same as those of girls and give up trying to improve.

Truth is, however, most professional writers are male, which made sense in the past, when women were not expected to have careers. Even though the overwhelming number of people who graduate from college today with degrees in English, journalism, writing, and foreign languages are women, there are still more men who earn a living as writers. You and your son need to be aware that males can make up the verbal difference and you should work on that. The bigger issue is why many boys make up the verbal disadvantage and girls are not as likely to make up the spatial disadvantage, but that is a subject for a different book.

Memory and Emotions

The hippocampus and the amygdala are small bits of the brain that also differ according to sex very early in an infant's development. If you drew lines front to back through your eyes and between your ears, where the lines crossed would be approximately where you would find these two brain structures. We have long known that the hippocampus is involved in helping us turn short-term memories into long-term memories. What has been recently discovered is that the hippocampus is a bit bigger at birth and enlarges faster in infant girls.

Does this mean that little girls have better memories than little boys do? Not necessarily, but combine this with the language skills of little girls and that may be why little girls appear to remember words better. Little boys have the reputation of not listening, but perhaps it is not that they are not listening; perhaps they simply don't remember words for very long. By contrast, they seem to have very good memories for what they see and do. For example, little boys don't often remember what their mothers tell them to do, but they will remember how to put a DVD into the machine just from watching someone else do it.

The amygdala helps us deal with strong emotions and to respond to emotions in others. This structure is a bit bigger and enlarges faster in infant boys. What this means is that little boys may have more forceful emotions than little girls have. When little girls get excited, they can use their verbal skills to express their emotions. If the little boys do not have strong verbal skills, they might be likely to use physical means to convey how they feel. Adults may pay more attention to the little girl who is excitedly talking about the upcoming visit to the zoo and less attention to the little boy who is expressing his excitement by running around pretending to be an elephant. In fact, not recognizing the little boy's behavior as a visible sign of his inner state, his emotions, an adult may tell him to quit being a problem and settle down.

Is it possible that little boys are more emotional than little girls? Again, not necessarily, but they are much more emotional than was previously thought and, early on, they do not have the verbal skills to communicate their emotions. Males have the reputation of being less emotional than females when, in fact, they are certainly as emotional; it's just that they do not express those emotions in the same verbal way that many women do. Emotional connection is extremely important for boys and, consequently, they won't work for a teacher they don't like (or they don't think likes them) or in a subject that bores them. On the other hand, they will work very hard—even if they are not doing well—if there is some emotional tie to the teacher or subject. Emotions have a huge impact for boys even if they won't admit to it.

The Senses

Everything we know, understand, or believe originated as information that came in through our senses. If there are differences in the ways boys and girls receive information because their sensory systems are slightly different, then that can help explain at some level the different ways in which men and women experience their worlds.

HEARING

At birth, children are given a test for deafness, and that test reveals that little boys are not as sensitive to sound as little girls are. That may be part of the reason why little boys are so loud and why they may find it difficult to hear whispers. Actually, little boys find it difficult to whisper at all: for centuries, mothers of boys have been embarrassed in quiet places like church when their sons tell them they "really have to go to the bathroom—NOW!"

Another problem for boys is that they are much more likely to have inner ear infections when they are infants. This sensation is similar to what happens when our ears are stuffed up when we cross over mountains or fly in a plane. These mostly viral infections during infancy usually don't last long and probably won't have any serious repercussions. However, these infections are most likely to happen during the period when children are learning language. Due to the combination of less sensitive hearing and viral infections, some boys don't hear the sounds of language clearly and may not develop *phonemic awareness*. That term refers to an understanding of the smallest bits of words. Having good phonemic awareness is the first step in learning to read. Additionally, if they are not hearing sounds, boys may not develop strong listening skills, and as you well know, listening is something teachers want their students to be able to do.

VISION

Just as there is a difference in hearing between boys and girls, there are also differences in vision. The first of these concerns the retina, the structure in the back of the eye that turns light waves into neural impulses. We know that the male retina is thicker than the female retina, but we don't yet know what that means.

Let's look at three other key ways in which the vision capabilities of the sexes differ.

1. Color vision: Males are much more likely to be color blind (a more accurate term would be color deficient) than are females. This is a genetically inherited trait that is far more common in males than in females. Normal color vision is called trichromatic because it involves cells in the retina that are responsive to red, green, and blue. Most color-impaired individuals, however, are dichromatic. Red-green color blindness is the most common, and there are several different levels of impairment. Some individuals see red and green as the same color—a sort of muddy, reddish brown— and others can tell the difference between red and green, but only if the colors are very strong. Blue-yellow color deficiency is much less common, and total color blindness, in which the individual sees only black, white, and shades of gray, is rare indeed. Young boys who are color deficient may be subject to derision by their classmates because they cannot tell the difference between red and green. Our color-blind son preferred to use blue and black crayons because

he knew what colors those were. And because most Christmas wrapping paper doesn't look very pretty to him we wrap his presents in blue and gold. In wrapping presents himself, he actually uses all sorts of paper on the theory that if it isn't pretty to him, the rest of the world likes it! On the other hand, he is not as fooled by animal camouflage as those of us with normal color vision are, so there are some advantages.

2. Gazing differences: Some research has discovered that neonates look at different objects. Baby girls appeared to be more likely to look at faces and baby boys at moving, shiny objects. While those findings are not very strong, there is supporting evidence. Adolescent girls are better able than boys are to get information from subtle facial expressions, body language, and vocal nuances, and men and women use different portions of the brain to process facial emotional information. This explains, in part, why a boy doesn't always get the message from an adult—especially if the message is a "look"—unless the message is very explicit and tells him exactly what he is to do. Evolutionary psychology explains the variance in gazing differences as stemming from the capacities early man needed to survive. Females needed short-range navigational skills and thus developed the ability to identify landmarks during the gathering of healthy food.

Males needed long-range navigational skills and developed a keen sense of direction for following game. The problem occurs when a young boy is directed to look at some object close to him, such as a book, and he may not be able to focus for long on a page. As he grows up, he will get better control over his visual focus. Gazing differences may be a factor in the later acquisition of reading skills by some boys.

3. Targeting: Another skill that boys have as a likely result of human evolution is their ability to hit a target with a thrown object. You probably have noticed that it is hard for boys just to drop an object into a trash can or a hamper. They have to ball it up, step back, and throw it as they would at a basketball net. Don't yell at them; they can't help it. Just make them pick up objects that didn't make it into the container and don't allow them to pitch objects that leak or come apart in flight (soda cans with a bit left in them come to mind).

TOUCH/PAIN

Telling your son to be "a man" about pain conveys that he shouldn't complain. But in reality, boys really *don't* feel as much pain as girls do. This is very hard to test, of course, but there are some indications for this observation. Take the case of quarterback Ben Roethlisberger, who played in Super Bowl XLII with two broken ribs, successfully throwing passes and helping the Pittsburgh Steelers win. As a football is thrown, the quarterback twists his torso somewhat so that he can use his whole body to propel the ball. Anyone who has had broken ribs will tell you that twisting your torso is not something you can do easily, but Roethlisberger either did not feel as much pain or was able to overcome the pain.

Little boys need to know this and to be encouraged to report their injuries. The reason so many do not do so is probably because adults are likely to overreact to small injuries. Boys know those little spills and bumps and scrapes do not hurt, so they learn not to react to all injuries. Let the child tell you how much an injury hurts. I have seen children fall and scrape their knees and not cry until some adult comes over and tries to comfort them. Just ask a child if he is hurt and listen to him. If he says it doesn't hurt and you have no evidence to the contrary, accept his verdict.

Staff in boys' schools report that boys need to touch others in developing a connection with them. This starts very early, and the place your son will be the happiest when he is an infant is in your arms. Yes, infants need to be in a safety seat when in the car, but once they are out of the car, they need to be touching you. Plenty of devices are sold that allow him to snuggle up to you, which he will prefer to the car seat. Actually, because he is in physical contact with you, you are more aware of him and he will be safer that way.

When I see parents carrying children in their car seats, it looks as if the child is being carried in a bucket.

And, while we are on the topic, when your infant son gets a bit older, resist the temptation to strap him to your front with him facing forward. Think about this from his perspective. He can't see you; yes, he can feel you and hear you, but he is hanging in the air and actually is encountering the world before you do. You will find that he will be a bit more comfortable on your back, where you are between him and the world, or simply in your arms where he can check with you about how he should be reacting to the world.

When he gets to the toddler stage, you may want to get a harness and leash. Okay, I know that sounds like you are treating him like a dog, but again, think about this from his perspective. Have you ever had to hold your arm above your head for a long time? Not very comfortable, is it? Well, that is exactly what a child has to do when he is holding your hand. No wonder he pulls away. Combine that with his interest in the world and your son will want to dart away from you. Putting a harness on him with a leash gives you security and gives him some freedom. Just ignore the glares from those who don't understand how great this arrangement is. Don't use the devices that connect the child's wrist to the parent's wrist. Those close with Velcro and it won't be long before your son figures out how to open the device.

Handedness

Part of touch involves a preference for hand use. Most individuals are right-handed, but left-handed individuals are more likely to be male. This makes sense because the right side of your brain runs the left side of your body, and the right side of the brain in boys develops early. Being left-handed is an advantage in some sports, such as baseball, but the world is built for right-handed people. It is really easy to teach a left-handed child to write or manage a knife and fork, though. Just sit in front of the child and have him mirror what you do. Make sure that when writing your son does not hook his hand around so that his pencil is in the same orientation to his body as it would be if he were right-handed. This is tiring, and the results do not produce smooth handwriting. Some boys do not settle on one hand or the other until first grade or later, so let your son try both approaches. Most of all, do not let anyone give your son the impression that being left-handed is a problem.

Dexterity

Most boys develop good large-muscle control early: the ability to throw a ball, run fast, jump in the air, or speak loudly, for example. What many boys have trouble with are activities such as coloring within the lines, handwriting, eating with a fork, or placing one block precisely on another. Boys will develop fine muscle control eventually, but they may need to start with tasks involving larger items. Your son may want to play with Duplo blocks long after age three, even though Lego blocks are for older children. The age limit is actually not for reasons of dexterity but because the smaller blocks constitute a choking hazard for very little children. Some boys will play with the larger blocks until they are five or six or even later. That's all well and good, but make sure your son practices fine motor coordination: teach him to put his toys away on a shelf, set the table for a meal, turn pages, hand you objects, and eventually to fold his clothes.

TASTE

When your son was very little, he probably ate pretty much anything you put in front of him—and sometimes things you would have rather he not put in his mouth! As your child becomes a toddler, he will stop growing quite so rapidly. When that happens, his appetite will slow down as well. If your child has begun to pick at his food, notice if his growth has slowed a bit. Here's a simple test to help you make that determination. When he was a baby, you had to get new clothes every couple of months or so, but now he can wear a shirt for half a year. That is a good indication of slower growth. If at the same time your child is not eating as much as he used to, realize that he probably doesn't need as much food any more. Many parents become extremely concerned that their child, who used to clean his plate, will not eat very much at this stage, and so they resort to bribes, treats, and special cuisines to tempt the child's taste buds.

Research has recently found that people who are picky eaters may actually have different taste sensations than do people who are willing to eat anything. So it may be that picky eaters are born, not made. Nevertheless, make it easier on yourself by *not* catering to your child's dietary whims. Do not ask your son what he wants to eat. He has no clue what is available, so he is likely to tell you he wants what he had the day before. But it won't be long before he will not eat anything except fish sticks and peas. Your child should eat whatever the rest of the family is going to have. You are not a short-order cook.

There are only five tastes: sweet, sour, bitter, salty, and umami, which can be called savory. All other flavors that we *think* we are tasting are actually the result of what we are smelling, which is why food doesn't taste very good when we have a bad head cold. Boys don't report being sensitive to as many smells as girls do, which you will discover to be a problem around early adolescence. At that time, your son may not be as offended by his body odor as those around him are, nor will he note that the dirty clothes in his hamper are beginning to fester.

So, when a boy dislikes a certain food, it may be due to the taste (it's almost certainly not due to the aroma), but it is more likely to be because of the texture. Many boys prefer instant mashed potatoes to the real thing because the instant variety is totally smooth. It doesn't seem to matter to them that when real potatoes are mashed with butter and milk, they taste better; boys don't like the lumps.

Food as a developmental hurdle

Let your toddler tell you how hungry he is. Make sure that you provide a healthy diet, very few if any snacks, and water and milk as his beverages.

When your child enters school, one of the major problems that teachers have is in dealing with children's dietary differences. If your child is not a picky eater, that will make his life in school a lot easier. Eating habits begin very early so that is why I am talking about what your child eats as a toddler. Also, poor diet is a major factor in how a child does in school and so the more that you can do to insure that your child eats a proper diet from the beginning, the more likely your child will be able to succeed in school.

Let me spend a little more time on the subject of snacks and treats. Plain and simple, do *not* provide many snacks for your son. Small children do better with five or six small meals a day rather than three large meals, but don't think of this as three meals with snacks. Your child may like a small bowl of cereal and milk at breakfast, followed by fruit (a third of a banana or a quarter of an apple), cheese cubes, and water mid morning. Lunch can be half a tuna fish sandwich, some green beans, and milk, followed by hummus on celery and juice mid afternoon. Supper can be a bit of what everyone else is having, plus milk. Chocolate milk should be a treat, not the normal way milk is served. It isn't that chocolate milk is bad for your child; it's that it is sweetened and he doesn't need the extra sugar. If your child won't drink milk, try cheese—real cheese, not cheese food. Many families serve fruit-flavored yogurt as a dessert. Lots of foods have calcium in them; consult the Internet to see what you can add to his diet. You can also ask your child's doctor about alternative milks such as soy, almond, rice, or coconut if your child will not drink cow's milk. Please remember that until your child is two years old, he should not have fat-free or reduced-fat milk because he needs the fat for healthy brain development. Also, look to see the recommendations for how much milk children need each day; it will probably be much less than you think.

If you offer your child a cookie, he is not going to turn you down, but that gets him in the habit of eating when he is not hungry. Do not bribe your child to eat or argue with him about how much he is eating. Either he eats or he doesn't. Part of the source for his struggles with you is that he is going through a stage where he wants to be in charge of himself, and now that he is putting food in his mouth this is an excellent way to gain some self-control. All a child should be required to do is to try one mouthful of everything on his plate. If he doesn't eat a meal yet comes asking for a snack later, he shouldn't get one. Your child isn't going to starve if he misses one meal. If he refuses to eat a meal and you give him a snack later, you have let him know you can be manipulated. Additionally, his "tummy clock" is now off and he will want to eat at times when meals are not prepared. That means he eats snacks. With the present-day problem of obesity in children, requiring your child to clean his plate or giving him snacks high in empty calories or high in salt only adds to this problem.

Food allergies are a major issue for schools. We really don't know why there is an increase in the numbers of children developing very serious food allergies, but it has become a real problem for teachers. Breastfeeding and waiting to introduce solid foods until children are at least four to six months of age are frequently suggested as ways to reduce incidence of food allergies. If you are concerned about this, check with your child's pediatrician for guidelines. Remember, children will eat when they are hungry, and just because you are hungry doesn't mean your child is also. It is a bit silly for parents and children to argue about what the child will eat. When your child does get to the stage where he wants to express his independence, it may help to give him a very limited choice such as which cereal he gets for breakfast or which fruit he gets mid morning.

Differences in Spatial Relationships

While girls have a verbal advantage early, boys have an advantage in some spatial relationships because of the early development of the right side of their brain. This may be why boys like to throw things; they can easily see objects in motion and they are developing the skills to hit a target. There are different types of spatial relationships, and boys are better at some while, in others, there is no difference between girls and boys.

Spatial-temporal is one of the types of spatial skills at which boys excel. It is the skill used in playing a computer game, that is, items moving in space at a certain speed. One theory is that listening to Mozart will improve a child's ability in this area. Granted, recent studies indicate that children who are exposed to music early, both listening and playing, do show an increase in intelligence, but not specifically in the area of spatial-temporal skills. Sorry, but there is no "Mozart effect."

Mental rotation, another skill at which boys shine, is the ability to correctly determine whether one three-dimensional object is like another one when the second one has been turned around. This skill is used when you can see that a wrong-side-up puzzle piece fits exactly into a space identical to the other side of the puzzle.

Disembedding is a third area where males have a distinct advantage. This is the ability to find one object in the midst of many other objects, such as locating one particular utensil—a slotted spoon, let's say—in a drawer full of other kitchen utensils. A simple test of this skill involves finding a simpler figure in a more complex one.

Can you find this shape in the more complex figure?

This is not the same skill as spatial perception at which girls are better. That skill is in matching similar items or in finding an item that is wrong; what is needed in proofreading, in other words. Disembedding involves finding a shape inside conflicting shapes. **Spatial perception**, a skill at which boys are somewhat better than girls, is the ability to find or compare objects while ignoring surrounding distracting information. Ponzi and Zolner illusions are examples of this ability.

Ponzi illusion

Are the two horizontal
lines the same length?

Zolner illusion

Are the three long lines
parallel or not?

Spatial visualization is an area where neither girls nor boys have an advantage. This skill involves mental manipulations of visual information that require several steps to resolve. Unlike the rotation skill, the individual pictures in his mind what something is going to look like after it is assembled or taken apart—but not turned around. How well can you pack a suitcase by considering what needs to go in and planning where objects should go before you actually put items in the suitcase?

THE PARENTS' GUIDE TO BOYS

Suggestions From the Teacher

As his parent, you are able to respond specifically to your son's developmental stages. This is where you help your son expand and grow so that he will be ready for what the world requires of him—school included.

READ TO YOUR SON

The single most important preparation for school for any child, boy or girl, is to be read to. For boys, whose early verbal skills are not likely to be strong, this is essential. If you do nothing else, read to him!

How often do you need to read to your child? EVERY night—no excuses. If you can't do it, make sure someone else does it. If there are several adults in the home (parents, grandparents, even teen-/college-age siblings and babysitters), they can take turns reading, and that way children can spend time with the adults around them in a quiet environment.

How long do you read? That depends on how old the child is. Very young children will probably be asleep after 15 minutes. Older children who are in school will want at least half an hour and some will want even more. Plan on half an hour.

How soon do you start reading to your child? A three-month-old doesn't understand what people are saying, after all. True, but children are paying attention to what is said around them surprisingly early. By the time a child is eight months old, he is babbling in the accents of those around him. Also, if you start the pattern of settling your child by reading before bed, you will find it becomes a habit that enables you to get your child to sleep at the proper time. Start the habit of books at bedtime very early even if you are only pointing out pictures.

When can you stop reading to your child? When your child tells you to, and not before. We read to our son until he was 12. The reason to continue reading to children who can read is that they become more fluent readers by listening. You will also find that the stories will bring up topics for conversation that you and your child might not cover otherwise. The last book I read to my son was *The Once and Future King* by T. H. White. My son was interested in why Arthur was mad at Lancelot and Guinevere and that started a discussion of infidelity. Talking about that topic as a part of a story meant that we could look at it with some objectivity. Also, it meant that my son knew his family's stand on that subject before he ran into examples of infidelity in the real world when he was older.

How do you read to your child? This is a more complicated question than it seems. The traditional method is for the child to be tucked up in his bed and for the parent to lie next to him or sit on a chair next to the bed. Some children will not sit or lie still to be read to. Let them sit on the floor in their pajamas and play with a quiet toy—building blocks work well. If you prefer to have your child sit in your lap, put the book in the child's lap and run your finger along the words as you read. At the very least, your child will learn two very important facts about reading: we read from left to right and from top to bottom. That seems like an easy lesson, but it slows a lot of children down at the beginning because they don't know the patterns. This also makes reading more active and interactive so that the restless child has something to help maintain his focus.

What do you read to your child? Go to your public library and ask the librarian in the children's section for suggestions. If your child does not seem interested in those books, ask mothers of boys what their sons like. Remember that boys like books with lots of action, even if it is a bit gory, and they like books that either are about real life or seem as if they are. They also love books that are silly. Your son will not learn to be violent by reading about violence as long as the book is appropriate for his age. I have read aloud lots of books I didn't like but my son loved. If you insist on reading books you like, you may not be able to keep your son's attention. For example, I loved the *Winnie the Pooh* books, but my son didn't like those stories at all. He preferred anything by Roald Dahl and Richard Scarry.

Why do you read to your child? *Why* reading is SO important involves several different areas. Reading develops the language skills necessary for a child to be able to read and it is through reading that a child can learn on his own. Reading allows a physical connection with parents that is not easily available during most of our daily interactions with each other. Reading is a habit that will help children settle down for sleep.

Language skills

Reading teachers know that in order for a child to learn to read, he has to become familiar with the sounds of his language. This is phonemic awareness. Until a child can easily understand every small bit of what people around him are saying, he can't easily learn to read. Even before children are born, they are listening to their parents, and a week or so after birth they can recognize the sounds of their parents' voices.

Why doesn't a child learn phonemic awareness from listening to the TV or radio? Have you ever misunderstood the lyric of a song? "There's a bathroom on the right" instead of "There's a bad moon on the rise," for instance. Lots of children think that the old hymn is about laundry day: bringing in the *sheets* instead of *sheaves*. All of us tend to hear what we are familiar with, and if there is no one to correct us, we make the same mistakes over and over again. Not only that, but if children were going to learn the sound of their language from TV, all the children glued to the set would have the accents of those on TV and not acquire the regional accents of their families.

Also, when you read to a child, you are in a quiet room with no distractions so you child can hear what you are saying more clearly. **I'm not an expert; wouldn't my child learn better from a recorded book?** No. Your child wants to please you and so he mimics you. Children have no connection with the guy on the CD, and because there are so many different accents, there is little continuity with pronunciation. Also, your presence helps your child focus on what you are saying. If he is listening to a recorded voice, he can get easily distracted.

Physical connection with parents

Attachment is the connection that children have with those who are important to them. These days, many children spend less time with their parents than they do with other caregivers or with teachers. In most households, when we get home, a lot of time is spent preparing a meal, eating, and cleaning up afterward. Those tasks are followed by doing homework or watching TV or working on the computer. Reading to your child gives him your undivided attention and lets him know you think he is important. I know you think you get that message across to your son, but recall that boys don't learn well from facial expressions or subtle expressions of affection. Boys need tangible proof that they are important to you, and spending time with your son is the best way. He actually needs physical contact with you as part of developing an attachment. And remember, this only counts if you do it regularly.

Boys frequently will not unload their deepest secrets when you are looking them in the face. When your son is old enough, you may find that you are more likely to get the real story if he is sitting in the back seat of the car than when he is facing you across the dinner table. Reading to your son probably means that you are not looking directly at him, and you may be surprised what he will tell you while you are next to him with a book.

Settles children to sleep

I'm always fascinated when parents talk about how hard it is to get their children into bed. My son occasionally would even go to bed a bit early because he wanted us to start reading to him. Routine is very important to children: "bath, teeth, bed, books" is the best way to prepare them to get ready to sleep.

And new information reveals that bright screens such as those on a TV, computer, or other electronic devices that can be read in the dark can prevent, or at least slow, the production of melatonin in the brain. Melatonin is one of the substances believed to help us go to sleep. The child who is glued to the TV or a computer game is quite right when he says he is not sleepy because the light from the screen is preventing his brain from making melatonin. Take him away from the screen, read to him a little, and you will be surprised at how easily he will fall asleep.

The importance of reading

The first skill that children learn in school is reading. After all, literacy rate is one way to judge the sophistication of a country. If you read to your child every night you get across these ideas:

- I think you are important and I'm willing to spend my time with you. In addition, this gives us some topics of conversation so that we can get to know each other.

- I think reading is important and you know that because I'm spending time reading to you.

- I think reading is fun and I want you to enjoy it with me.

- I'm a responsible parent and I follow through with my promises to you. You can trust what I say.

TURN OFF THE TV AND THE COMPUTER

According to information in a 2007 issue of *Archives of Pediatrics and Adolescent Medicine*, 90% of 2-year-olds watch TV regularly and 40% of infants who are three months old watch at least an hour a day. Another article in the same issue indicated that regular TV watching was associated with toddlers and preschoolers developing attentional problems as well as learning difficulties. A 2007 study in the *Journal of Pediatrics* found that watching TV did not lead to an increase in language development. In fact, for children 8 months to 16 months who were just beginning to speak, more hours in front of the TV reduced their language development whether or not the program was intended to be educational. (On another subject, a more recent issue of *Archives of Pediatrics and Adolescent Medicine* revealed that infants and toddlers who watched TV instead of sleeping were more likely to be overweight.)

What this research means is that TV for little children is not good. Yes, they will watch it and it keeps them quiet, but it is not giving them any benefits and may do harm. Especially do not let children under two years of age watch any TV; they simply sit in front of the screen like vegetables and do not get involved with what is going on. So not only is watching TV a waste of their time, it is a waste of their brains and the most important point made by the research is that watching may actually slow down learning. If there are older children in the house, they should not be watching TV when the toddler can see the screen.

What about programs for the computer or TV that promise to help your child learn better? The cited research specifically indicates that children who are exposed to those programs don't learn any better or faster than do children who haven't used those programs. In fact, the only factor that predicted an increase in verbal skills was *the amount of time the child was read to*. What your child needs is YOU!

TALK/SING TO YOUR CHILD

Some of my earliest memories are of listening to my mother sing to me when I was sick. True, she had been a trained vocalist who after years of not practicing had lost some of the beauty of her voice, but she was a believer in singing to children and those memories are precious to me. I can't tell you if one reason our son became a singer was because his father and I sang to him at bedtime and with him in the car, but it certainly didn't hurt. We all have fond memories of singing "The Wheels on the Bus" as we drove down the road on a family trip.

We not only sang to our son but also talked with him. From the day he came home, I carried on absurd conversations with him when he was in his bath, when he was nursing, and when we were on walks together. Both my husband and I talked to him as if he were an adult, and it was not long before it was obvious he was charmed. What sort of things did I say to my son? (Remember this was long before he could talk or even understand what my husband and I were saying to him.) "Oh, do you see the bird that just flew by, that is a blue bird. It is a lot nicer than the blue jays in our yard; remember I showed one to you yesterday?" After he babbled a bit, I'd add my two cents' worth. "Oh, do you really think so? It never occurred to me that might be true. Where did you read that—in the paper?" Then he would babble a bit more. By the time he could talk, he knew the rules for conversation. I talk, you talk, then I talk again, and so forth. He knew that your voice rose a bit at the end of a question and went down a bit if you were being forceful. He was used to talking to adults; I know he wasn't actually talking, but we treated him as if he were.

The most important point to remember in all of this is

Don't talk baby talk to babies!

If you need to talk baby talk, get a dog. One of the ways that children learn to talk is to listen to those who talk to them, and if the conversation is in baby talk that is what the child will say. This can be a bit embarrassing when an older child cannot pronounce simple words correctly because those around him have been speaking baby talk, and it certainly is going to create problems when your son gets to school. His teacher will not know the family pet name for bodily functions and may have a hard time understanding what he is saying. The result can be that boys simply learn not to talk a lot in school and that will negatively impact their ability to learn.

And while we are on the subject, don't use what I call a "parentese" voice with boys: you know, high and light, the typical voice people use with baby mammals. Remember, boys aren't as likely to respond to high or soft sounds, so they may not pay attention to what you say. You don't want to use a very loud voice, either; just a normal inside voice.

How soon do you need to talk to your child?
All children will begin to babble around three to four months of age. At that time, they can make all the sounds the human tongue, teeth, lips, and throat are capable of. So at that point children speak every language. By the time a child is eight months old, his babbles are limited to the sounds of the language he hears around him. That means you need to be talking regularly with your son from the beginning. Just because he can't speak does not mean he isn't listening.

Have you ever noticed children misbehaving in the grocery

store? It is pretty obvious that the child is screaming to get the mother's attention. Watch the mother: she rarely looks or talks to the child; she is totally absorbed in her task of finding what she is looking for or talking to someone on the phone. That is the reason why children begin to demand items. After all, mother is taking stuff off of the shelves, why can't the child have some of that also? And, when that ploy doesn't work, the child starts to stand up in the buggy or to scream.

All of this could have been avoided if the mother had just talked to the child as she did her shopping. "Let me see, your father wants oranges. Well, look, there are three different types of oranges," she says as she points them out to her son. "Some of these don't look very orange and the ones that do are very expensive. Oh, look there is a bag of oranges of the type he wants. Don't you think he will like these? Let's get him a bag."

By the time your child is two or three, he can help get groceries. Did it ever occur to you to notice that favorite cereals are on the bottom shelf? By the time my son was six, he could pick out good bananas—not too green, not too ripe—and find most of the items I was looking for. If they were above his head or too heavy, his job was to point them out to me. The only time he fussed was when I was spending time talking to someone else. One day when I was going on and on, he reached up, grabbed my face so I would look at him, and said, "It's time to talk to me now." We then had a discussion about interrupting adults and what sign he could give me that it was time for me to move on. But he knew that going to the grocery store meant he had a conversation with *me* and therefore he had my attention.

START SETTING BOUNDARIES

Discipline is one of the major topics that teachers discuss. If you want your son to succeed in school you need to make sure that he can control himself at the level expected for his age and grade. That will change as he grows up, of course, and he should know what the expectations are for his behavior at each level.

It is important for you to understand that your child does not see discipline in the same way you do. What you see as an appropriate disciplinary response to misbehavior may not matter to him, and what you think is unimportant may be vital to your child. Remember also that for little children the world is a huge and unpredictable place. The boundaries you set are comforting to him; they mean that you care enough to keep him safe. You are an adult, and you set your own boundaries. Your child does not know how to do that, so even if he screams or complains, remember that he needs those limits and that it is your job, as his parent, to provide them. And yes, you will say, "Because I said so!"

The art of parenting is all about knowing what boundaries to set and when to move them. The boundaries that are appropriate when your son was 3 will not be appropriate when he is 13. You should also remember that what is cute at 3 may be illegal at 13, so don't let a child get away with bad behavior just because he is little. You may think he doesn't know what he is doing, but it is more likely that he does know the behavior is not acceptable. He may not know why taking a cookie is not right, but he knows he shouldn't do it.

Little boys don't seem to respond well to an appeal to pay attention to others or to others' things. For example, saying, "Don't do that. How would that make you feel if someone did that to you?" doesn't get much response from many boys. On the other hand, they should learn to respect the possessions of other people, especially those in their family. That goes two ways, of course. Their possessions should also be respected. So if a boy damages part of the house or another child's toy, he should apologize and, when old enough, offer to fix or replace the object. His possessions should be protected from his siblings as well. No one should be allowed to get away with purposeful damage.

When do you start?

You start setting boundaries when you realize that your child is engaging in purposeful behavior. And you know that because he looks at you after he does it (to see your reaction). At the beginning, a child is fascinated when he drops things from a high chair and they always fall down. Eventually, he will figure out that if he drops stuff he gets your attention, and then the dropping becomes purposeful. It is still a basic science experiment that is lots of fun, so he isn't going to stop it. In this situation, you need to learn to pick your battles. Get a splash sheet to go under the chair. But let him know that throwing things (as opposed to knocking them off the tray) is not acceptable.

What Can You Expect From a Toddler?

Most children are well behaved in most situations and that is a credit to both them and their parents. When children are prepared for a situation—"We are going to the grocery store now. What do you think we will find today?—they are much better able to deal with events as they happen. When children are not prepared, they can react badly because they are not sure what is going on. A lot of what is seen as bad behavior is actually the result of a child's difficulty in maintaining self-control. Preparing him, talking to him, and modeling behavior will all help your child learn what is expected of him in various settings.

In disciplining your child, it is not necessary to yell at him to get him to behave. Being very firm and consistent will get better results. Time-out does not work very well with some boys. If you do use it you will find that you need to stay with him to ensure that he stays in the time-out location. It works better for you to remove him from the situation. With boys, you need to very clearly point out which behavior is unacceptable: tell him exactly what he did that was wrong, and what you expect. Do not lecture him. Believe me, his feelings will not be hurt when you treat him in a straightforward manner.

Here are five key behaviors any parent should expect of their toddler:

1. No throwing objects not meant to be thrown. If your son throws food, simply remove the food from in front of him because it is a good indication he has finished eating. If he objects, tell him he can have the food back, but it is to be eaten, not thrown. If he continues to throw it, and he will, take the food away, wipe him off, and take him out of his high chair. Other thrown objects are similarly taken away.

2. No standing up in high chairs, car seats, and grocery store carts. If he gets up in his high chair, take him out and take the food away. He will learn that if he is hungry, getting food means sitting down to eat. If he unclips the buckle on his car seat, stop the car as soon as it is safe to do so and do not go again until he is buckled. (My husband was very slick in handling this issue. When our son figured out how to unclick the belt in his car seat, my husband would hear that little click and drift the car over to the side of the road. "Oh, my," he would say. "I don't know why the car stopped. Son, did you unclick your seatbelt because you know the car won't go if everyone's seat belt is not fastened?") If your

son stands up in the cart at any store, take him out and leave the store. Take your son outside and tell him you will go back inside the store when he assures you he will stay seated. It is crucial for children to stay seated in these three situations—high chair, car seat, and cart—for safety issues. Also, if you can maintain your authority in these matters, you will find he will mind you in others. (By the way, your toddler probably doesn't want to be in the grocery store. For a while, it may be easier for you to find someone to watch him while you shop.)

3. No screaming or running around in public places. My mother always said that she would not allow my brother and me to bother other people, and I carried that out with my son. If he screamed, we left, no matter what we were doing. It doesn't take long for your child to realize you mean what you say so don't think that you have to do this forever. Some preventative measures also help. When we knew we would be going to a place where our son might be tempted to scream or run around, we would get him to run beforehand. And I've seen lots of parents in airports playing with their children in the unoccupied parts of the concourse where they are not bothering anyone because shortly thereafter the child will have to stay seated while in the airplane.

4. No biting, scratching, or injuring other children or animals. This is a huge issue for children in daycare, and it's one which you as the parent are best able to control. If your son begins this behavior tell him it is not allowed. If he continues, remove him from the other children. He is the transgressor so he is the one to go. He should also apologize for hurting the other child. Do not tell him to say that he is sorry, because it is very likely he is not sorry for what he did; he is only sorry that you caught him at the behavior. He can learn to apologize even if he can't say the words "I apologize" very well. He must also learn not to hurt animals because they are likely to return the behavior. Cats and dogs are not stuffed animals; they are other living beings that need to be respected.

5. Putting away his toys. He doesn't need to be neat about this, and having a large basket for his toys is probably the best solution. It is easy to see and retrieve items out of a basket with no lid. If he takes the toys out, he can put them back. He will need your help, at least for a while, to know what to do, but make a game out of it: "Mommy/Daddy puts one in and then you put one in." By the way, if you make your child put his toys away, you have to tidy up yours as well.

What do you want your toddler to be able to do?

- Listen to directions and follow them.

- Sit when required, especially when standing is dangerous.

- Respect other people and other people's things.

- Begin to be responsible for his actions by starting to put his things away.

CHAPTER 3

INSIDE A BOY: PRESCHOOL
AND KINDERGARTEN

You've got the brain of a four year-old boy, and I bet he was glad to get rid of it. —Groucho Marx

When I grow up, I want to be a little boy. —Joseph Heller

At this point, for most of your son's life he has been either at home or in day care. In any case, he has been doing pretty much what he wants to do. If you are lucky enough for one of you to be a stay-at-home parent, your son has had a lot of attention from one adult. If your son has been in day care, he has shared adult attention. The ratios differ from state to state, but generally the standards are one teacher to three infants or one teacher to four toddlers. If school-age children are present, that may change the ratios somewhat. In any case, infants and toddlers in day care should be getting the same amount of adult attention they might get from a parent—with the advantage of fewer household chores to distract the adult.

The Outside World

If your child has been at home he should have had some interaction with other children, perhaps his siblings or children in your neighborhood. Socialization of children is very important, so if your child has not been with other children this is an important step. Please know that your son needs for you *not* to be part of his interaction with other children. For a while now, you have been getting down on the floor and playing with your son. When he's four and five years old, it's time to step back and let him learn how to get along with other children. DON'T HOVER! You want your boy to become independent, and if you do not give him some freedom, he will be living in your basement playing video games when he is 30 years old! If you are wondering how that happens, it starts here.

"But," I hear you say, "he and the other children fight and yell, he cries, and I have to take him home. The only way they will play nicely is if one of the mothers plays with them." Children have to learn the boundaries of what is acceptable behavior. Your son has no idea that what he does hurts other people, and the only way he is going to learn is if he and other children cross each other's boundaries in roughhousing. Little children are egocentric, which means they see the world only from their viewpoint. Part of growing up is the realization that other people do not share your view of the world. If your preschooler was at home with older siblings, they would be doing this all the time and you would simply tell them to stop it and not tease their little brother.

That does not mean, however, that you let him and two other boys loose in your family room unsupervised. It means that the little boys should *not realize* their parents are watching them. They do need to be watched to make sure that nothing dangerous happens, such as swinging an object at someone else or throwing hard objects in the house. Preschool-age children don't actually play together; they play alongside of each other, so they can be unaware that what they are doing is impacting—literally—others in the same area.

Brain Changes

We know that as we grow and interact with the world, our brain changes. And, it changes differently depending on the experiences we have. How much does our life affect us? We really don't know, but remember from the discussion in Chapter 1 that when identical twins reared apart are compared on various measures, they are closer than are fraternal twins reared together. Who we are is determined more by what we bring to the environment than what the environment does to shape us. Identical twins reared together are not totally the same, so differences in experience are important, but we probably have less effect on children than we think we do.

LATERALITY

Recall from the previous chapters that the differential development of children's brains may explain why your son may have been a bit later to speak and use language fluently than a similarly aged girl, but that your son was better able to throw objects accurately and to run rapidly. Why is rapid running a boy trait? One theory is that the right side of his brain is developing faster than that of a girl so he may be able to deal with rapid oncoming visual information a bit better. That may also be the reason why he may have better targeting skills.

By the time your son enters kindergarten, the left side of his brain is starting to catch up to the left side of girls' brains, but most boys are still a bit later in developing and using verbal skills. Those differences can be the basis for social and disciplinary issues for boys in school. One trait that contributes to the problems boys have in school is that boys are highly competitive. Since this is seen in boys around the world in a wide variety of cultures, the temptation is to believe that competition is brain based, but there is no evidence for this. In any case, girls are competitive as well, but in different ways, and they may take failure more personally than do boys.

Boys, on the other hand, are pragmatic. If they don't believe that they can win and that no amount of work will help them, they simply will not try. Remember this in the future when your son tells you it's useless for him to work hard especially if he believes that a teacher does not like him. He will not compete if he does not feel there is a reasonable chance of his success. So, if a boy is substantially behind girls in verbal skills when he enters school and his school focuses on reading and speaking, he may not put forth much effort at getting better in areas that he believes are stacked against him. He will focus on physical activities that are more clear-cut and, based on what he has learned from those around him, are areas in which boys are supposed to be successful.

If a boy is behind a girl in developing the verbal skills so important in school, would it be better to hold this boy back? The research on this is not very clear. Some research says that it makes no difference in the long run; other research says it makes a large difference, especially for boys. If your son falls into this category, talk to the teachers at his school to see what they recommend. Do not worry about keeping him up with his friends at this point. Holding him back at age 4 or 5 is preferable to having to do it when he is 10 or 15, a time when he will resist the notion so that he can stay with his friends.

Holding a child back in preschool or kindergarten is not the same as failing, and it doesn't mean that the child who is held back is not intelligent. It means that the child is not ready for the academic activities that make up much of the program. You wouldn't let most 5-year-olds play soccer with a group of 10-year-olds because the younger child's body isn't ready to compete with the older children. The same considerations apply when a child does not yet have the skills required to manage school. He will develop those skills; he just doesn't have them now. And to put him in a class he is not ready for means he will be convinced he will never be able to do the work, just as the 5-year-old playing soccer with older children is convinced he is no good at the game.

VERBAL SKILLS

By reading and talking to your son you have been helping him develop his verbal skills. He is also stretching his verbal abilities by talking with his friends when they play. You may notice, however, that even though boys speak much louder during play than girls do in their conversations, the boys actually talk less to each other. Two little girls playing with each other will constantly describe to one another what they are doing and include the other in their play. A typical statement from a girl might be, "I'm going to make this and then we can put what you are making together with what I'm making." Boys, on the other hand, will work side-by-side on a building project and may inform each other what they are doing, but they don't converse about what the other is doing. A typical statement from a boy might be, "I'm building a car and it is going to be really big."

Boys working together on a large project such as building a fort will decide on various jobs and then do them independently. One of the reasons that they don't really like girls playing with them at this stage is that they see the girls as being bossy. "She tells us what to do" is a common complaint. The girls believe that the job will progress better if each participant communicates what he or she is doing, but the boys don't work that way.

COGNITION

At this stage, you may be surprised to find that your son is finally beginning to understand that what is inside the TV is not real. For instance, Big Bird is not really somewhere between three inches to a foot tall (depending on the size of your screen). He may still think that what happens on the show is real, however, even if it is a cartoon. Very little children do not know the difference between cartoons and reality. Even somewhat older children can be confused if a character on a show goes away and then they see a rerun and the character is back again. Remember the earlier discussion about not letting very little children watch TV at all? This information indicates why you should limit the amount of time preschool children watch TV programs as well.

Keep reminding yourself that children *do not think like adults*. If you don't believe me, try this simple demonstration: Get two glasses that are the same size and a third glass that is taller and narrower. Put the same amount of water in the identical glasses and add food dye to make them different colors. Ask your child whether each glass contains the same amount of water. Then, in front of your child, pour the contents of one glass into the narrower glass; the level will now be higher. Ask your child again whether the amount of water in each glass is the same. A child under six will tell you that there is more water in the taller glass even though he has seen you pour the identical volume of water into the thinner container. The point is that children of that age cannot keep track of several different qualities of a substance at once. Don't correct your child. He will learn over time that the volumes are the same even though they are in different shaped containers. This is the same reason why young children think that taller people are older. My point is just because you understand what is going on in a TV show does not mean your child has the same understanding. Remember, you and your child see the world differently.

The experts will tell you that children of this age engage in magical thinking and that they believe in animism, that is, inanimate objects such as toys have life. This isn't surprising, knowing that *Toy Story* movies and *Monsters, Inc.* are so popular. Try to think back when you thought your toys talked to each other or that there really were monsters in your closet. Don't try to dissuade your child. Why? Because you won't have much success, and this way of believing is part of the basis for imaginative and innovative thinking that will be necessary later on in life.

When our son had nightmares, my husband would go in to comfort him. One of their rituals to help our son deal with his fear of the bad dreams was to have him whisper a really good thought into his father's cupped hands. My husband would then ball up his hands and slip them under our son's pillow saying, "Now you have good thoughts that will go into your brain and chase away the bad ones." Pure magical thinking, but it gave our son the confidence to go back to sleep certain that the bad dreams would be replaced by good ones.

The down side of magical thinking, though, is that your son may be scared of Santa Claus or the Easter Bunny. You may want the traditional picture of your son sitting in such a seasonal character's lap, but he may be terrified to be so close to this personage who in his mind has so much power. If you take your boy to the mall for a picture and he says NO, don't force him. Perhaps he will let you take a snapshot of him with Santa in the background. Know, too, that children this age can be frightened by clowns, especially those whose makeup is very elaborate. Why? Because this is exactly what they are afraid of: their toys have come to life and now are hugely bigger than they are. At some level small boys and girls understand that toys shouldn't come to life and this just seems wrong somehow.

Another aspect of magical thinking means believing that objects do not always have to follow the basics of physics. Some youngsters believe at some level that people and objects can fly, and these boys and girls may actually try to do so themselves. Lots of little boys have broken an arm falling off the garage roof in an attempt to be Superman or Harry Potter. Magic won't mean much to a child who is already convinced that things can just appear and disappear. Pull a coin from a little child's ear and he may cry because he didn't know he had money in there. A rabbit being pulled out of a hat isn't surprising because the child doesn't understand that the hat isn't supposed to be big enough to contain a rabbit. Consequently, it can be upsetting to have clowns or magicians entertain at parties for little children.

Emotions

Around this age, children become aware of their own emotions, but most do not have many words with which to express those emotions. Little children generally express only three feelings: happy, sad, mad. One thing you can do for your son is to expand his emotional vocabulary by helping him acquire words that are variations of these three basic emotions. For example, it will help him to know the difference between mad, angry (which is a bit more than mad), and upset (which is a little less than mad). When your son says he is "mad" at you, ask him if he is mad, angry, or upset. The discussion will distract him and he will learn to be clearer about what he means.

Research indicates that early in school some boys get into more trouble than girls do because they cannot express their emotions clearly enough for the teacher to understand what is going on. So the teacher sees an upset boy and assumes he was responsible for the incident, when it may have been the other child's fault. But simply because the victim didn't have enough vocabulary, he wasn't able to let the teacher know what actually happened.

In addition to being limited in how they express their feelings, boys are not very aware of emotions in others. When you look at someone's face and are able to understand what emotion that person is feeling, the part of your brain responsible for that recognition is called "mirror neurons." Initially, research indicated that mirror neurons click on early in females and might explain why adolescent girls are much better at reading body language than are boys. More recent information is not so sure of sex differences in this part of the brain, but the gender difference in the skill still exists. If you say to a boy, "Don't do that! How would that make you feel if someone did that to you?" he hasn't a clue. It seems as if boys are not empathetic, but the problem is that they don't read emotions. Boys are concerned about how other children feel; they just may not be able to figure out what is going on with their peers.

To help strengthen this development in your son, tell him how it makes you feel when he does something. Don't expect him to figure it out. Say, for example, "It makes me upset when you don't do your chores." Men complain that women don't tell them what they are feeling, and women complain that it is perfectly obvious to someone who is paying attention. So, women assume that men are not paying attention, but it is difficult for men to read emotions. Emotions are important to women, but they need to get that across to men. Don't make them guess.

The Senses

As children grow, their senses become more experienced and they do a better job of managing the information they receive from their environment.

HEARING

If your son does not seem to be paying attention to the sounds around him, one issue may be that boys respond primarily to voices and music. They really don't hear noise. (Girls at this age respond to voices, music, and noise.) If your son is throwing a ball against the house, don't complain about the noise because the noise doesn't bother him. Instead, point out the damage done to the paint on the wall or the potential of breaking an adjoining window. Soft foam balls exist so that boys have something to throw that doesn't drive their mothers wild. These balls don't fly very fast, however, so your son won't be satisfied with one for long. Put up a hoop and realize that there is some comfort in knowing where he is by the thump, thump, thump of the ball against the side of the garage. It won't be long, Mom and Dad, before he will be gone.

VISION

You might not be aware of your eye movements when you read. But as your eyes go across this page, they continuously dart forward just a bit so that you know what is coming up. Those movements are called saccades, and if you only read one word at a time, you might find it hard to actually figure out what you were reading—particularly if the sentence was somewhat lengthy. So, your eyes go forward and back just a bit. We know that at least part of the difficulty for some individuals with serious reading problems is that their saccades are large, so large, in fact, that such people lose their place and can't find the word they are supposed to be reading. At the very least, these readers tend to miss short words and the endings of words. There is some evidence that some boys may have larger than normal saccades, but not large enough to cause identifiable reading problems. Nevertheless, this movement may interfere with a boy learning to read. As the boy matures, he will gain more control over his eyes and the saccades will not be as great a problem. (Note that in some people the problem of large saccades seems to diminish as they age, but some folks have the problem all their lives, and they have serious dyslexia as a result.)

EFFECT OF SENSORY CHANGES

If male and female children have differences in their brain development and in their senses, how do these differences affect the way they think or process information? Aren't boys and girls able to learn just about the same material? Yes, but not always in the same way and not at the same time. That is the problem in school for children who are either early or late developing or whose skills are very different from those of everyone else. Taking into account what is different between girls and boys, the average boy is likely to:

- Need people to talk directly to him and to speak firmly; not yelling, just not softly.
- Need help in learning language and be given lots of opportunities to be engaged in language activities.
- Need those around him to understand that he is likely to be emotional without necessarily being able to verbalize those emotions.

- Respond quickly to visual stimuli and loud noises.
- Require tactile stimulation to learn, but at the same time, be less likely to feel pain.
- Learn better from what he sees and does than from what he hears or reads.
- Be easily able to find his way in his world and need to use those skills independently.
- Need clear directions about behavioral expectations.
- Need physical assurance from caregivers; yes, hugs, but also other forms of physical closeness.

Other Developmental Hurdles

In the paragraphs that follow, I've discussed behaviors we believe are true of boys, but for which we cannot find a specific brain response. I believe that most of these are a combination of biology and environment because they are not necessarily absolute. In other words, many boys will show these behaviors, but others will not.

KNOWLEDGE RECALL

If you have ever watched the television show *Jeopardy*, you will have noticed that a large proportion of the champions are men. There are several reasons for this: males have more fast-twitch muscles than females do, allowing them to hit the button a bit faster; males may be more competitive; but most importantly, males are trivia nuts. There is even solid evidence that for pure recall of facts, males are better at this than females are, but only when the subject interests them. This is why, among other reasons, the *Guinness Book of World Records* is so popular with young boys. They love to be familiar with such obscure facts as the world record for numbers of jumps on a pogo stick.

This ability frustrates both boys and their teachers. Plainly the boy can remember; after all, he knows all the pertinent information about the players on his favorite team. Then why can't he remember the dates in his history lesson? Simply put, he cares about the first and doesn't care about the second. It doesn't help if the teacher presents most of the information by lecturing. When boys are allowed to get involved in a lesson, they are more interested. Lots of techniques are available for teachers to use to improve the hands-on aspects of lessons.

NEED FOR MOVEMENT

Boys need to move. There is some biological evidence for this in that during puberty, boys have a higher average metabolism than do girls. That is why they are always hot and they can eat huge amounts of food and not gain an ounce. But even before that, boys appear to need to move more. When comparing children of different cultures, this early need to move does not seem to be universal, so some of this may be coming from our expectations of the energy level of boys. "Boys will be boys" frequently follows an event in which something was broken as a result of a boy running around in the house. When biology is added to expectations, some boys appear to be unable to sit still.

Does this mean you should make your little boy sit quietly? Probably not, but it may mean that you can require him to sit longer than he thinks he can. If you expect him to be able to do it, he may. Also, look at how long he sits quietly while he is doing something he is interested in. The problem is likely to be boredom, not necessarily a case of the fidgets. Be realistic, no boy will sit still without something to do; provide fiddle toys, small squeezable objects, or simple games.

On the other hand, young boys do have a lot of energy and they need to wear it off. When your son comes home from school, the first thing he needs is some exercise. If you have a back yard or a nearby park where he can play, that's great. If you don't have space, one solution is for your child to be enrolled in an after school organization that provides lots of activity. Most importantly, do not let your child sit immediately in front of the computer or TV. Yes, I know it means he is quiet, but it also means that when he is in school, he may have too much energy. One other thing you can do is to give your child subtle ways to exercise. Use exercise balls of the appropriate size for chairs in front of the computer or TV. Keeping his body upright on the ball develops core strength, and he can wiggle on the ball and it won't break or make noise.

AGGRESSION

Aggression is a kind of competition where the individual is determined to win. No question about it, boys are more aggressive than girls are, and this is not learned behavior. It is true all over the world. This is a trait of males and they should not be made to feel guilty because of it. However, they should not use their aggression as a way to control others. That's what bullying is, basically—aggressive behavior designed to threaten another. You need to teach your son early on that winning does not mean you hurt others in your desire to be first. On the other hand, celebrate with him when he does win fair and square.

Bullying

Bullying is traditionally a problem of middle school, so why bring this up now? The reason is that the patterns of behavior that result in bullying or victimization start as soon as your child encounters other children, and that is happening at this stage. However, don't think that all aggression, either by your child or directed at your child, is bullying. Boys are aggressive; that is part of what makes them boys. But schools are particularly sensitive to this issue. You have certainly seen reports in the media of a wide variety of bullying behaviors and are aware of what can happen.

At this stage, aggressive behavior by boys is not usually purposeful and therefore is not bullying. However, if a little boy is allowed to use his physicality to get his way with other children, that can set the stage for future bullying behavior. It is a real art to know how to help your son learn how much aggression is acceptable or how to defend himself against an aggressor. Many children have no problems with this give-and-take on the playground, but the child who does have problems may need help learning social skills. If this is the situation with your son, alert his teachers when he gets to school.

How do you keep your child from becoming a bully? Children will resort to bullying when adults are not around, when they see others bully or are bullied themselves, and when they are taught that bullying is not all that bad. You need to provide good supervision and teach your son how *not* to become a victim. Also make sure that no one in his immediate environment resorts to such tactics to get their way. I don't mean that you shouldn't use your status to make him toe the line. You should resort to the "I'm the mother, that's why" admonition now and again because you are not trying to hurt him. Yes, he may cry if you are firm about his behavior, but that is out of frustration. If your child misbehaves at home but not in public that is a great compliment to you as a parent. That means he trusts you.

If someone accuses your son of being a bully, take a deep breath and don't defend him until you know the facts. Most parents of bullies are totally unaware of how their son treats his peers because he knows how to behave in front of his parents. It is entirely possible that your son is innocent, but it is equally possible that your son is guilty. If you have reason to believe that your son is bullying other children, please seek help for both of you. Do not let him get away with the behavior, especially if he learned it by being bullied himself. Let your son know that the behavior is unacceptable, that it will stop immediately, and that there will be serious consequences if it continues—and stick to your guns.

The most important thing you can teach your child is how to respond to a bully. This is another place where your intervention will not help your son. He has to learn to defend himself. If you intervene the other children will see him as someone who cannot protect himself, and he will be even more vulnerable. It is important for him to understand that the bully is actually not very sure of himself, which is why he is attacking others. The best defense is not to engage with the bully, so your child may need to learn to avoid that child or learn not to respond. The child who does not respond is no fun, and the bully will move on to find a more responsive target.

Little children are easy targets because they are so accepting of behavior by older children and adults. Additionally, they are easily threatened because they don't understand that an older child does not have the power to hurt his parents. (A common threat is, "If you tell, I'll hurt your mother" or "If you tell, you'll be in trouble.") It can be hard for little children to tell someone about the abuse because they are frightened. I have no magic elixir to protect your child, but keep the lines of communication open and know your child well. If his behavior changes, it can well be due to the fact that he is growing up, but if his behavior becomes less mature or he begins to act out, be alert to the possibility of bullying. Change his schedule where you can so that he is playing with a different group of children and see what happens.

Roughhousing

One other form of aggression is playfighting, what is also known as wrestling or roughhousing. This isn't fighting or bullying. If you ask your son to stop fighting, he will rightly tell you he is not fighting. One way to tell the difference is whether fists are involved. Fists indicate real fighting, and that must stop. Pushing, pulling, rolling around on the floor are all roughhousing, usually accompanied by giggles or loud boasting. Yes, boys can and will get hurt, and that is part of the game. If it does become real fighting, don't worry; tomorrow your son and his pal will have forgotten all about it. Research indicates that this is normal behavior for young males— both human and four-legged. This may seem odd to mothers who see this as mean or strange. This behavior is not usual in females unless they have brothers, in which case, sisters sometimes do roughhouse with their brothers.

There are two rules for roughhousing: (1) only two combatants, and (2) if someone says stop, the game stops. You will see grown men doing this with their brothers or other men they are close to. Many women just see this behavior as dangerous.

There is one other important point to know about roughhousing:

Boys Need To Roughhouse

You can't really stop them—it's native to the human animal—and if you try, it just means they will do it in places where adults are not around. In fact, letting boys wrestle at home in a safe place is optimal. This behavior is analogous to what I see at home. My two male cats, who are brothers, have been roughhousing all their lives. They are big enough now to knock over small pieces of furniture and to leave the rugs in my office askew, but after one of these episodes, they will curl up together for a nice nap.

WHY DO BOYS HURT OTHERS?

Preschoolers and school-age boys really don't mean to hurt others, at least at the beginning. Boys are impulsive, active, aggressive, competitive, and physical, and they have no idea what effect their behavior has on others. This behavior is, for the most part, not learned. Boys come into the world this way. Some boys learn to moderate their behavior and others get worse. Your job as a parent is to help your child learn the boundaries of acceptable behavior.

How you do that is counterintuitive. Boys learn acceptable behavior through roughhousing, which to remind you is NOT fighting. As I said earlier, boys *need* to engage in this activity. In fact, research has shown that boys who engage in rough-and-tumble play have better social skills than those who don't. The reason is simple: the other child will complain when the play gets too rough and may respond in kind. If one child bites, the other may bite back, and both learn that biting is unpleasant. (Obviously, biting is not an acceptable part of roughhousing.) If you prevent your son from this sort of play, he will engage in wrestling when he is older and you are not there to stop him. At that point, he is much bigger and can actually hurt someone else. The point of letting little boys wrestle is that they are not likely to actually do much damage, but they *will learn* the limits of acceptable play.

Little boys should not watch professional "wrestling" or other extreme fighting sports. They will learn unacceptable moves and positions that actually might cause real damage. Make no mistake, boys don't really want to watch wrestling; they want to do it. Watch a boy who is watching pro wrestling; he will try to mimic the moves with the family dog! So give boys an acceptable place to play and go away.

Your son is learning what the boundaries of acceptable behavior are, how far can he go before he hurts someone. He really doesn't want to hurt his friend, but boys like physical closeness. If your son's school prohibits wrestling on the basis that it is fighting, you have two options. Tell your son that he cannot engage in wrestling in school and that he and his friends are welcome to come to your back yard for that behavior. The other option is to talk to your son's teachers about whether the school will allow the boys to wrestle during recess or see if the school can add some similar activity in PE class.

PAYING ATTENTION TO OTHERS

One of the most frequent complaints I hear from teachers and parents is that boys do not seem to have much empathy for others. This complaint usually results when a boy has hurt someone else and doesn't take responsibility for the injury. You will remember from earlier in this chapter that mirror neurons are the part of the brain that is used when you are trying to figure out what someone else is feeling. One theory is that these cells are not very active in boys and thus many of them have a hard time determining emotions in others. There is some concern that this may be part of the problem with autistic children who are not aware of the feelings of others. Boys are usually genuinely concerned when they understand that someone has been hurt, they just don't often do a good job of figuring that out on their own.

How do you teach a boy to have empathy? You don't, but what you can do is teach him to respect others. This will result in his treating people in a way that doesn't create problems. The golden rule is problematic for a boy to grasp because when he is little, he has no idea of the effect his behavior has on others. Without seeing how his behavior impacts others, he cannot determine how that would make him feel.

This is why parents are sometimes tempted to spank boys. They suppose that spanking will get through to him that the consequence of his behavior is something that hurts him and others.

So what about spanking? There probably isn't one parent on the planet who hasn't thought about that practice. Critics argue that a spanked child learns to respond with hitting and research indicates that may be true. After all, the child thinks, if Mommy or Daddy hits me, then slapping or striking others is an acceptable way to get them to do what you want them to do. Certainly that does happen, and I've heard children shout to one another words that convey, essentially, "If you don't do what I say, I'll hit you!"

No matter what you do to discipline your son, it is important that you show him that your unconditional love does not depend on his good behavior; you want him to behave well because it is safer and kinder to others. "Hate the sin, but love the sinner" as the Good Book says. Be specific when you discipline your child. "No throwing blocks in the house" sends a different message than "You are behaving badly" does. He can change whether he throws blocks, but he doesn't think he can be good all the time.

Recent research indicates that there may be long-term serious effects of spanking. Mood disorders, major depression, and alcohol and drug abuse were linked to the use of corporal punishment. This research indicates a link between the disciplinary method and long-term results, which does not mean that one causes the other, but there is certainly some link. Until the experts sort this out, it is probably best to find some other method to discipline your son. No matter what discipline method you choose, you should know that successful parenting is a matter of consistency more than anything else. Most importantly, both parents should agree on the method of discipline used. This never works if parents disagree. In that case, the parents might consider a family counselor to help them sort out the situation.

Suggestions From the Teacher

As his parent, you are able to respond specifically to your son's developmental stages. This is where you help your son expand and grow so that he will be ready for what the world requires of him—school included.

INCLUDE YOUR CHILD IN FAMILY DISCUSSIONS

What I have in mind here is that everyone, no matter how young, participates in the conversation around the kitchen or the dining room table. A classic example is the Joseph Kennedy family, which required even the youngest child to take part in discussions of political or academic matters over dinner. As you well know, that family produced a president, an attorney general, and a senator. Children need to be able to talk to anyone, and the safest place to start learning that skill is at home. Additionally, it gives parents a venue in which to shape their children's beliefs.

Not every family eats dinner together at a table. In fact, the habit for many 21st-century families is for everyone to grab something and eat in front of the TV. Research points out, however, that children who eat family dinners do better in school. Why should it matter to your academic success where you eat? The theory is twofold. First, families that eat dinner together tend to have regular schedules that are enforced. Learning to keep to a schedule helps children be better students because they do assignments regularly. Second, families that eat dinner together talk to each other. When parents and children talk, parents know what is going on with their children and can provide assistance when necessary. Also, children who are eating with their parents are a captive audience for a while and have to listen to what parents are saying.

Don't ask your child questions such as "What did you learn in school today?" That question results in either a grunt or the one-word answer "Nothing." Ask your child questions that require him to think about the day before answering. You can ask a young child, "What was the silliest thing anyone said today?" or "What happened today that you found surprising?" As your child grows up, you can require him to read one article in the paper and report on it to the family. The article can be anything from a sports item to the lead article on the front page. One child whose family employed this strategy remembered trying to push the envelope on what was considered an article. He used the classified ads and reported on the cost of purebred puppies. He remembers his father then asking him how did the price of those dogs compare to the cost of the other dogs advertised for sale and how many total ads for dogs were there. In retrospect, he knows his father understood what he was trying to do, but wanted him to understand that if he was going to try to slide out of his obligations too easily, then harder requirements would follow.

The art of conversation

It is the job of parents to make sure that children are well prepared for all of the eventualities in life. Learning how to talk to anyone and acquiring a wide knowledge of the world will provide children with the tools to get along in the adult world. Children who do not have this skill lose out because adults will focus on the child who is making an effort to get along with them. That is also true in the workplace, where a boss is likely to focus on the employee who can convey a message clearly and succinctly. Some business schools today are finding that they need to teach their graduates the art of conversation.

In school, the child who can talk easily to adults is often perceived to be academically capable by teachers. One study pointed out that little boys who could not effectively get their point across to teachers were more likely to get into trouble in school. It was not that the children could not talk; they were just not used to telling someone else how they felt or what happened to them. Parents are much more willing to give a child time to figure out what he wants to say, and that patient listening and urging will help the child learn to express himself.

CHORES

You remember chores, those jobs that everyone in the family had that kept the household going smoothly? Garbage detail, lawn mowing, washing dishes, scrubbing the bathroom, and walking the dog to name some of the most common ones. As we got older, we were more and more responsible for ourselves: laundry (at least our own); fixing meals (either our own or helping with the general family meal); going to the grocery store; picking up siblings from practice; and the like. The idea was that chores taught you to work, to be responsible, and to be an active part of the family. So what happened to chores? Most of my middle and high school students do very few chores, if any, and usually only those directly involving them. Their parents continue to pick up the slack.

It's so slack that several of my college students still can't make a bed or do their laundry properly. One of them came to school in a formerly white shirt that had been washed with something dark colored. When one of his fellow students commented on the shirt, he said he had no clue why that happened. I asked him what temperature the water was that he used. He looked surprised and told me that he washed his clothes in hot water to kill the germs. So I stopped my class and conducted a short lesson on the basics of laundry. After class, several other students came up and asked if I could help them figure out other basics, such as making their bed. One student slept in a sleeping bag because he didn't know how to make a bed with sheets, and another student, who lived in an apartment, complained that it really didn't save him any money over living in the dorm because he didn't know how to cook and so ended up eating out most of the time.

What concerns me about these students is not that they could not cook, clean, or look after themselves, but that they had no idea how to go about figuring out how to learn. They had no idea how to find out that information on their own. I pointed out that they could ask a fellow student, they could ask their mothers, or they could seek the information on the Internet. None of those solutions had occurred to them because they had never had to do anything on their own before. Everything had been prearranged.

That approach to life—wait for someone else to do it or to tell them what to do—influenced their work in school as well. They were always able to do what their teachers required, but they had no notion of how to approach the subject differently or how to figure out a solution on their own. That creates an attitude of dependence that will haunt them all their lives.

I get the feeling from some parents that they want their children to remain dependent on them, or to put it another way, they think that having independent children means they have been bad parents. In fact the opposite is true. The successful individual is very independent and thinks and manages on his own. Encouraging independence is the hallmark of the good parent.

How soon should children be given chores?
The wonderful answer to this question is "As soon as they can pick up their toys and put them back in a toy box," and that may be as young as 18 months. At that age, it is not their responsibility, but they should be involved. For the parent, it would be easier of course just to put the toys away without the child's help, but that is not the point. Parenting is about teaching, and the sooner your child learns that if he takes toys out he is responsible for putting them back, the better.

Try implementing in your home these "Golden Rules for Living," which you can find all over the Internet:

1. If you open it, close it.
2. If you turn it on, turn it off.
3. If you unlock it, lock it up.
4. If you break it, admit it.
5. If you can't fix it, call someone who can.
6. If you borrow it, return it.
7. If you value it, take care of it.
8. If you move it, put it back.
9. If you make a mess, clean it up.
10. If it belongs to someone else, ask to use it.

Do you realize that if everyone puts away what they take out, there is nothing to clean up? This is all about responsibility, and if your child is given the chance to be responsible, he will develop a sense of self-respect that will take him through life. Those who are responsible for themselves can be trusted to follow through with assignments.

What are chores children can do? You should be able to trust a three-year-old to pick up his toys and put them away, to set the table for a family meal, and to pick up sticks in the yard. Picking up sticks is a huge help to whoever mows the lawn, even if it is a lawn service. As children get to be kindergarteners, they can put their clean clothes away, make their bed, and dry dishes/empty a dishwasher.

Do not excuse your child if he fails to complete his chores and do not do them for him. If your three-year-old fails to set the table, everyone sits down to eat as usual. Do not yell at him if he fails to put out the knives and forks; let your child realize for himself the consequences of not doing his chores. Someone may say, "Oh my, how are we going to eat? What do we need to be able to eat our meal?" And, every now and then, thank your child for completing his chores successfully. You don't need to thank him every time, but often enough so he knows you notice that he is doing what is expected.

Children need to feel that they are a part of the family, and having chores helps that attachment. It is not mean to make children do chores. Parents who require this kind of involvement know that it takes time to learn to be responsible and that the responsible person is happier.

Should you pay a child for doing chores?

Parents don't get paid for doing what they do around the house and for the family, and neither should children. It is part of the responsibilities that come as a member of a group. You should tell your child every so often how well he is doing his chores and explain how his work saves you time and energy.

Your preschooler probably doesn't need an allowance yet, but you need to be thinking of this. What you don't want is to get in the habit of doling out money every time your child asks for something. Having an allowance gives your child control over what he spends. Whatever the going rate is in your neighborhood, give your child a little less. Not a lot less, but just enough so that he can make up the difference by doing something extra for which he is paid. That is called incentive. Every child should have a budget that includes saving some money each week. Then when he wants something special, he will have the extra money available. He should also be encouraged to give some of his savings to the charity of his choice or donate his time toward that charity.

Very young children do not understand the value of money and it is your job to make sure that your child develops that understanding. Even if you can afford it, do not give your child everything he asks for. Children need to learn the difference between what they need and what they want. You will provide everything they need, but little of what they want. Close friends raised their son this way. The following anecdote shows the effect it had on him.

My friend and I took our two little boys one year to visit Santa Claus. We stood in line for a long time listening to children list all of the toys they hoped to see under their tree. Finally it was my friend's son's turn to sit in Santa's lap. When Santa asked him what he wanted for Christmas, the little boy looked at him with astonishment and said, "Presents!" I noticed that this family may discuss what they need and methods to obtain necessary items, but the only things they talk about that they want are intangibles such as success. Gifts are just that, and are not to be asked for. Obviously, that lesson had registered with their little boy at an early age.

While we're on this subject of remuneration, don't pay children for grades. The practice will work for a while, but it won't last forever. Research found that people worked for money only when the task involved simple physical skills. For higher cognitive tasks, pay only resulted in people doing worse, not better. Eventually your child will realize that the money is not worth the work and he will whine for more money. What you want to do is to get the child to realize the intrinsic rewards in doing well in school. Your job is to help him learn that, and the lessons start early. People do best when they are self-directed. Again, this may be a bit early to be thinking of this topic, but start out as you intend to go on. Even preschoolers get some sort of grades or marks.

In my home, we thank everyone for doing anything for us. I thank my husband for taking the trash out and he thanks me for fixing a button on his shirt. We don't make a big deal of it, but if I'm at my desk when he is emptying trash cans I'll say "thanks" as he does that. It is an acknowledgment of work done as well as providing a value for the work. If your three-year-old hands you something you dropped, thank him. When our son's grades in school improved, we told him we were proud of him. Extrinsic incentives such as money work only as long as the incentive exists; intrinsic incentives such as having pride in what you do last forever because the value is yours.

Remember, everyone does chores, not just the children. Sharing the household tasks translates into more time for the family to do things together. More importantly for a boy, he feels that he is a member of the family group. Boys need to belong to groups and being a member of his family is very important. If you don't help your son see his place in your family, he will find another family, such as a gang, to be a part of.

TEACH YOUR CHILD TO PAY ATTENTION TO OTHERS

As your child grows up, it becomes more and more important for him to pay attention to the people around him. It can be very irritating to others in public when a four-year-old is loud in his insistence that he get a toy or certain food. One flight I was on, for example, was actually held up because the parents were unable to convince their son that he absolutely had to sit in his seat with his seat belt fastened before the plane could take off.

Teach your child to apologize to others when he inadvertently bumps into someone or comes between them and what they are looking at (a good skill in the grocery store). It is important for boys, who are very physical, to understand that their behavior affects others and to start learning how to manage themselves in public.

TEACH YOUR CHILD NOT TO INTERRUPT OTHERS

You are the most important person in your son's life, and he wants immediate access to you. If you don't respond because you are talking to someone else, he does not see that it is rude to interrupt. Teach him how to recognize when you are talking to another adult and develop some family signal for him to let you know he needs your attention. Once you realize that your child needs you, excuse yourself and turn your attention to your child.

When you are with your child, be careful not to spend a great deal of your time on the phone with others. That is disrespectful to your child; it says to him that his presence doesn't matter to you. And your behavior might be the source of some of his misbehavior. If you find that your child acts up when you are on the phone, see what happens when you keep your calls short. Talk with your child instead; you may be surprised at how much you find out about him. Part of teaching your child not to interrupt is not to interrupt him. If he is talking with anyone else—child, parent, teacher—treat him with the same respect that you want from him. Use the same family signal to let him know that you need his attention.

DISCIPLINE

If you find yourself saying, "I get tired of saying 'no' all the time," then your discipline methods are not working. Telling a child "no" isn't sufficient. Here are the steps to disciplining a boy:

1. Decide what is not acceptable behavior for your four- or five-year-old. You and the other adults who are in charge of the child need to agree on this list. Items on the list might be: bedtime is 8:30; no throwing things in the house; no damaging things that don't belong to you; no hurting other people; and the like. Make sure that the list is short and general so it will cover most eventualities. Please also make sure that the list is reasonable and takes into account normal boy behavior. No child will be completely quiet all the time, boys probably less so than girls. As your son grows up, you will have to add items to the list, but make them general. When items are added, make a big point that this is something new on the list.

2. Use the 1 – 2 – 3 and you're out strategy. My husband taught me this and it works a treat.

a. The first time your child does something you do not want repeated, you drop down to his level, have him face you, and tell him: "That behavior [be specific] is unacceptable. Do not do that again."

b. When he does it again, and he will, drop down again and say: "I told you not to do [that specific thing]. If you do it again, this is what will happen [again, be very specific]. (By the way, DON'T say, "Remember, I told you . . . ?" That comes under the heading of questions you already know the answer to.)

c. When he does it the third time, apply the consequence. The great thing is, it won't be long before your son knows that you are serious and that if you directly tell him not to do something, he had better not. It means you won't have to keep saying no.

Here's a firsthand example that illustrates this to a tee. One day we were at the playground and the kids started throwing sand. I told my son to stop. He did it again and I told him that if he continued, we would go home. He threw sand again. We hadn't been there five minutes. I gathered all our things and told him we were going home. "I won't do it again," he protested. "I know you won't when we come back tomorrow, but today we are going home." The best part about this method is that you stay in control and don't lose your temper. This method is for behavior you want stopped, but once your child realizes you are serious, he will pay closer attention when you tell him no.

3. Don't sweat the small stuff. Just because the behavior bothers you, it may not bother others. I mean things like wiggling a leg at the dinner table (that actually helps a boy learn to control himself) or wearing mismatched clothes. Take a deep breath and let him do it.

4. Make sure that your child knows it is the behavior you object to, not him. "Hate the sin and love the sinner." One boys' school corrects boys by pointing out that they have made wrong decisions and that if they had made a different decision, there would be a different outcome.

5. Make the consequences reasonable and fit the crime. Going home from the playground was reasonable and told my son that I wasn't going to allow him to pitch sand. It said to him that I thought he could learn to control himself because we did go back the next day. If your child continues to kick the seat in front of him in a movie theater, leave the movie. It is not the end of the world; you can go back the next week to see the movie. But by preventing him from continuing to do

what he was doing, you are teaching him to control himself. Part of that teaching is giving him alternatives. If he is kicking the seat in front of him, suggest that he kneel on his seat instead.

6. Don't argue with your child. You are the adult and you are in charge. The next time you are witness to a parent-child argument, note how as the parent gets louder in an attempt to make his or her point, the child gets louder and eventually they are screaming at each other. Learn to use a firm, supported voice at the beginning that says you are in charge. It may sound mean to you, but to a boy it says you expect to be paid attention to. What do I mean by a "supported" voice? Listen to people who sound like they expect to be listened to. You will find that they speak from the diaphragm rather than from their upper chest. Their voice is supported by the diaphragm. It isn't a louder voice, it just sounds more authoritative—and children pay closer attention to it.

7. Don't try to sugarcoat the message. If you want your child to stop, say so. If you say, "Honey, I wish you wouldn't do that," he thinks he has an option to continue. "Stop doing [be specific]" is all that you need to say.

As you read these steps in disciplining a boy, did you say to yourself, "That sounds so mean!"? If so, my response is this: it is no meaner than a cop telling you that you are not allowed to speed. The point of good discipline is that you don't have to use it very often. If your child knows you are serious and that you are paying attention to him in the first place, he won't resort to misbehavior. And this isn't martial law, either, because you are reacting to *what* he does. This isn't a set of rules that *proscribe* his behavior.

Some consequences that work

In the past, parents have used physical consequences, but children of this age are too old for this sort of punishment to be appropriate. We have recently learned that forces that torque the head, brain, and neck as a result of blows or slaps to the head can create huge damage, which may be permanent. A tap on the back of the hand of a child who is reaching for something forbidden is acceptable as long as the adult understands the effect of the force applied. It may be just as effective if you simply put your hand firmly on the child's hand to stop him from reaching and accompany that motion with a definite "No."

Time out is the most often suggested method to impress upon a child that the behavior is unacceptable. I mentioned earlier that time out doesn't work well for boys, and it is also less effective with older children. It can work for kindergarten-age children if it is a method of last resort and not something that happens on a daily basis. If you leave the child, it is too easy for him to get up and do what he likes, so you must stay with the child. Find something to do so you do not engage your child in any way, but make the time out stick.

Consequences must be immediate in order to work. "Wait until your father comes home" never was much of a deterrent. Most of the methods that do work involve you losing something as well: leaving a playground when you want to talk to a friend, leaving a movie, leaving the grocery store, and the like. However, let me reassure you that if you are firm and convincing, you won't have to do this often. If you find that these methods don't work, you are not doing one of two things:

1. You are not following the "1 – 2 – 3 and you're out" rule and are letting your son have "just one more chance."

2. You are not paying enough attention to your child. If you are on the phone and your child misbehaves, that is not entirely his fault because the behavior may have been designed to find out if you were paying attention to him.

Most importantly, decide what is serious enough for you to forbid it. Just because your child is annoying is not reason enough to make him stop. If he is racing around the house making a lot of noise, he probably needs to do that, yet I agree that may not be appropriate inside behavior. If you let your child behave inappropriately indoors, he will never learn that he should change his behavior according to his location. That's what makes the notion of "inside voice" and "outside voice" so clear. You can certainly apply that to activity as well, but you must regularly give him the chance to use his "outside voice" and "outside behavior." If you don't have time to give your child regular outdoor exercise, make sure that he is enrolled in some program that will. Otherwise, he will be loud and boisterous in school and that will certainly get him in trouble.

Remember, your child may be escalating his activity and noise in order to get your attention. Pay attention to what you are doing when your child misbehaves. If you were otherwise occupied, the misbehavior may simply be a ploy to get you to notice him. A child who is constantly bothering you is not good either. This is the time when the old standby works so well. "You are bored? All right, how about you help me clean the house? You can be in charge of dusting all the undersides of our chairs and tables."

As your child grows up, you will find that he needs some alone time as well. A child who is constantly around his parents will depend on them to entertain him and that may be the source of his annoying behavior. Children will do better later when they can play by themselves for a short period of time when they are young. If his misbehavior is an attempt to get your attention, suggest to him that he play by himself. If he finds that difficult, and children of this age may, set your kitchen timer for ten minutes and tell him that when it goes off, you will do something with him. I bet that when the bell rings, you will find him engrossed in an activity by himself.

The key to discipline

In order for your son to learn self-control you have to trust that he will learn how to behave. If you are always there, he can't learn that, so you have to give your son space in which to make mistakes. Don't be a helicopter parent, that is, one who hovers. In fact, research is clear that the best adjusted and behaved children have parents who provide strict guidelines and are alert to their child's activities, but they let their son or daughter make mistakes. Parents who are restrictive and psychologically controlling have children with more behavioral problems because the children never learn how to behave properly and appropriately on their own. The children of helicopter parents behave when their parents are around, but they fall apart when the parents are absent.

What do you want your preschooler and kindergartener to be able to do?

- Continue to develop verbal skills.
- Begin to learn that behavior is site specific; a behavior might be acceptable in one place and not in another.

- Compete fairly and lose gracefully.
- Understand that his behavior affects others and not to be unkind or mean.

CHAPTER 4

BOUNDARIES
(HIS, YOURS, EVERYBODY'S):
ELEMENTARY SCHOOL

There comes a time in every rightly constructed boy's life that he has a raging desire to go somewhere and dig for hidden treasure.

—Mark Twain

I pay the schoolmaster, but 'tis the schoolboys that educate my son.

—Ralph Waldo Emerson

For some time now, your child has probably been interacting with people outside of your family. He has likely been to nursery school or kindergarten, and it's time for him to be off to elementary school. He knows this is different; before, it was just play, but this counts.

Another issue is that your child is going to be judged by others. It can be a little scary to have someone assessing his ability to follow directions, his manners, his physical attributes—let's face it, his intelligence. This is not a reflection of your parenting skills, but it is going to feel that way every now and then. You want the world to see your son for the fascinating, funny, and stellar boy you know he is, and it can be difficult when the world does not totally agree.

As a teacher of boys and as a mother of a boy who was not a total success as a student, I've been on both sides of this situation. Some of my students had parents who simply refused to accept the notion that their child had learning issues or was the source of major problems in the classroom. Some of my son's teachers were convinced that his learning problems required solutions that my husband and I were not comfortable with. As with all such disagreements, the best path is to get several different opinions. The hardest lesson to learn is that you may not be able to personally solve your son's problems, but your job is to find the person who does connect with him to enable him to respond.

I've been there and I know very well that parents can be blind to their child's shortcomings. That doesn't mean that you have to accept everything others say about your boy, though; they can be wrong. But if several different sources are giving you the same basic message, you may need to reconsider how you see your son. It is going to feel as if you are directly responsible somehow. That is great when your son is a success, but his accomplishments are no more under your direct control than are his failures. Your child is a genetic mixture of two people, which means he is not a clone of either parent.

This all boils down to it being a bit difficult when you see your own shortcomings in your child. What you want to say to him is, "Don't do that. I know that approach won't be successful because . . ." Sorry, but your child will probably have to learn the hard way just as you did. You can't protect your child from the world, nor should you totally. I know you hate to see your child suffering or having to struggle to learn a lesson you also learned the hard way, but if you are proud of how you turned out, let your child learn in a similar fashion.

Because your son is not exactly like either of his parents, he isn't going to react the same way either of you do. Also, what works at home may not work elsewhere. You are going to be surprised at some point that he responds to an approach you never thought of or that you never believed would work with him. Parenting is a series of surprises, both positive and negative, and the best parents learn to roll with the punches.

Brain Changes

As your son grows up, the changes in his brain slow down, which may mean that changes in his behavior are less obvious. They are happening, however. Think about the difference between first graders and sixth graders and you may get some perspective on what is happening to your child.

VERBAL SKILLS

At the beginning of elementary school, many boys are still substantially behind girls in development of verbal skills. That is why the first several years of elementary school are spent making sure all students can read and why a great deal of the material is presented in visual form. When the approach of schooling changes and there is a shift from learning to read to reading to learn, some boys will still not be ready for the change. When that happens, a boy who previously loved school may change his mind and now may be reluctant to do his work, may refuse to be cooperative in class, and may even resist going to school. His parents are going to get a lot of notes from the teacher, and the end result will probably be a conference with the teacher, the learning specialist, and someone from the administration. At some point, the child will be referred for testing to see where the problem lies.

If the boy has been doing well in most of his work up to this point, chances are that his problem is no more serious than being behind his class in developing verbal skills. The ability to read has become the benchmark for a child's academic abilities, and the child who is behind the curve may be identified with learning issues. It will come as no surprise to you to know that the overwhelming majority of children around the world who are identified with learning disabilities are boys. It seems as if being male puts one at risk for learning problems and that does not make a lot of sense. Why would one sex be more likely to have trouble learning, especially when they don't seem to have a disproportionately greater probability of failing to succeed in life skills?

Some experts are convinced that the differences are due entirely to expectations; in other words, the environment—especially teachers—assumes that boys are going to do poorly and consequently they do. We know that the differences in brain development that were so apparent at birth are now very small, but they still exist. Remember that research on adults indicates that males and females do not process verbal tasks in the same way. There is no question that much of what happens in early school tries to help boys develop verbal strengths, but the differences are still there.

Sensory Changes: Vision

For the most part, boys have more acute vision than do girls, especially when objects are in movement. Nevertheless, there is one part of vision at which girls are very good and boys are not. This is called "perceptual speed," and it involves skills that are necessary to pick out one different object among many similar ones. Recall from the discussion in chapter 2 that there are differences in spatial skills between boys and girls. For example: circle the picture that is not like the other ones. This is something that children are often asked to do in elementary school, and it will help if you let your son know that he can do the task if he slows down. Help him look for cues to differentiate the pictures from each other. Give your son the large Richard Scary books to help him find Goldbug, or get the *Where's Waldo?* books to give him practice in locating specific pictures among others.

This skill is necessary in proofreading and is a partial explanation for why boys can't always locate errors and why they don't like to check their work. If a boy will read out loud what he has written, he will have better luck in finding his mistakes. Even if he talks out loud to himself as he locates the different picture or characteristic that will help.

Other Developmental Hurdles

As I mentioned earlier, it is somewhat puzzling why so many more boys than girls are identified with learning problems. It is a possibility that the cause of this difference is the way many boys learn, which may be at odds with the way they are taught. Think about it. Teachers were probably good students—after all, they like being in school—and most of them believe that good students listen well, read well, and are attentive. That type of learning is described as verbal and auditory. Yet a little boy is much more likely to learn from pictures and by doing. That type of learning is described as iconic and kinesthetic. Your son learns well, but not in the way the teacher is teaching. That is the reason for this book, to help you help your son acquire some of the behaviors that will give him an advantage in school.

Education used to define the word "normal" much more broadly, but with the advent of high stakes testing and national educational standards, the definition has narrowed. Additionally, every child is expected to succeed academically even when the child has no interest in or aptitude for academic achievement. Many boys used to succeed in school by preparing for such trades as plumbing, electricity, and car mechanics. Students in those fields learned language arts through business letters and contracts, math through accounting and bookkeeping, and history through studying civics in preparation for being small business owners. Now, however, children are not allowed to take the trade courses until they have mastered the academic courses, even though those who would be interested in learning a trade may find most academic courses difficult or irrelevant. Many of these students simply fail to master any education and end up in dead-end jobs.

I'll get off my soapbox now, but if your son shows promise in mechanical reasoning and hands-on learning, do what you can to give him the opportunity to shadow someone in the trades. If he is struggling to read, he may gain some confidence in knowing there are other areas where he can succeed.

LEARNING DISABILITIES

These are behaviors or conditions that make it difficult for any child, not just boys, to learn. The language-based disabilities are more common in boys probably because of their slower left brain development. There is a difference between problems of late development and serious learning disabilities, but it is very difficult to make that distinction early in school. As long as the late-developing child understands that his problem is one of maturity and he will be able to read well before long if he just keeps at it, then there is no difficulty in labeling a developmental reading problem as a disability. On the other hand, if the school leads the child to believe that his reading problems are due to some permanent disability, he may not even try to read. What concerns me is that the boy may well be able to learn if he is offered a different approach. If that works, then what he actually has is a learning difference. Educators have come to believe that there are best ways to learn and see these differences as disabilities. One thing that you can do for your son is help him believe in his ability to learn in his way.

I am so sure about this because of all the men I know who have told me they became good readers after they left school. As long as they were in school, they were treated as if their brain was broken for reading. When they left, there was no one to make them feel bad about their reading skills, they found reading material that interested them, and the reading part of their brain matured. I know a boy who could not read in first grade and was a poor reader in third grade, but by sixth grade, he was a superior reader. It was a developmental problem, not a permanent disability. His improvement occurred when he went to a boys' school where being a poor reader wasn't a huge issue. He was given books to read that he found interesting and discovered that reading was something that boys liked to do. Schools will tell you they understand this, and in truth the help they give is usually appropriate. But the underlying attitude toward the reading issue makes the child feel that his brain is faulty and that he cannot improve.

Four categories of learning disabilities are most commonly cited as having gender differences.

Attention Deficit Hyperactivity Disorder (ADHD)

The medical community does not define the category of ADD (attention deficit disorder) anymore. The categories are ADHD, Predominantly Inattentive Type; ADHD, Predominantly Hyperactive-Implusive Type; and ADHD, Combined Type. In 2013, the guidelines for diagnosing these conditions will change and may revert to just two types, ADD and ADHD. In any case, there will be changes in how the disorder is identified. The idea here is that the child cannot sustain attention and therefore cannot learn. The belief is that there is some difficulty in the way the child processes information, and there is a growing body of evidence to demonstrate that there are differences between the way the affected brain and the non-affected brain work. However, research does not agree on the cause, and the more scientists look, the more they disagree.

Often, educators at a boy's school will identify him as having one of the forms of ADHD, and his parents will report that he seems to be able to pay good attention at home. If that is true, then there are several explanations for the differences.

1. He may not learn well by listening. Go into any classroom and you will notice how much talking the teacher does. A child who does not have good auditory memory may be paying attention to what is happening in class but be unable to repeat what is said. This is one of my problems, and I've had to learn to take down everything the teacher says; otherwise, I can't remember it. Also, the child with poor auditory memory may have learned that there is no use in paying attention to what is said because he knows he is not going to remember it. Having poor auditory processing is also described as a learning disability. My point is that it is only a disability if the teacher does a lot of talking. In the science class I taught at a boys' school, there was no textbook, and I used only about three to four minutes at the beginning of class to show the students how to set up the lab exercise. Once the lab was finished, all the data went up on the board and everyone in the

class participated in a discussion of the results. There was no book that explained what students were to do or helped students figure out why they got the results they did. Students who have a hard time learning by doing could be said to have had a learning disability in my class because they have a kinesthetic processing problem. (I did provide some auditory, visual, and tactile learning, of course, but those styles were in the minority.) In all classes, the teacher needs to supply information in several different ways.

2. He may be bored. The bright child can get the point of the lesson fairly quickly, but when the teacher either repeats the material or gives more examples to help students who don't understand as quickly, he starts to think of other things. Pretty soon he gets wrapped up in his own thoughts, and when the teacher moves on, the quick learner is not paying attention. If the entire class moved at a quicker pace, the child would have no trouble keeping up.

3. He may be not interested in the subject. Remember, boys learn well what they like. If they don't like a subject or they think the teacher does not like them, they won't work.

One of the other symptoms of ADHD is hyperattention to a

123

subject. Let's face it, either a child can pay attention or he can't. If he is perseverating (focusing to such a degree that he is oblivious of what is going on around him) then the reason is more likely that he has finally found something that interests him. Educators have a hard time admitting that children may not be totally fascinated with everything that happens in class. I have a lot of the symptoms of ADHD, but I can spend hours doing research and writing about boys because the subject fascinates me. I have a lot of trouble paying attention when the subject doesn't interest me. I don't have a deficit in attention; I just don't care to manage my attention when I'm not interested. True, I don't have spectacular focusing skills, but I can do it when needed.

ADHD does exist, but it is much less common than the number of boys labeled with the disorder would lead you to believe. The most important point is that attentional issues exist in all facets of a child's life. If the only place the child has problems paying attention is in class, then his problem is not likely to be ADHD. If the only place the child *does* pay attention is while playing a computer game, he may well have ADHD. A child with attentional issues is not so much paying attention when playing such a game as constantly being stimulated by new information over and over again, which reconnects his attention to the screen.

A growing number of educators are interested in the subject of "engagement." What has been identified as a lack of attention may actually be a lack of engagement by a student. The information on boys' emotionality that was covered earlier indicates that they do work well when they like the teacher or the subject. What may actually be happening is that the boy is not interested in the subject and that looks as though he is not paying attention.

Dyslexia

This disability is the general category that captures all sorts of problems in acquiring information from words, in reading words, or in processing words. There are many different forms of dyslexia, and some are more disabling than others. Some forms are serious disabilities and will require years of remediation; other forms are simply due to later maturation of the reading part of the male brain. If the latter is the case, the support given these boys will help, but make sure that the boy understands he will be able to read well as soon as his brain matures.

Also, another cause for reading problems may be larger than normal saccades. (You might want to review the description of these movements that is in chapter 3.) There is a difference between the very large saccades associated with one form of dyslexia and the slightly larger-than-average saccades that have been found in some boys. Your boy will be able to control his eyes better as he matures, and some of the exercises provided by a reading specialist will help. If a child has serious problems acquiring information from the written word, the school may suggest that the child receives texts from *Recordings for the Blind and Dyslexic*, an organization that for a small fee provides recorded versions of textbooks. And don't forget, reading out loud to your son on a daily basis will help him acquire some verbal fluency.

Dysgraphia/Dyspraxia

The first term, dysgraphia, is part of dyspraxia, which is the more inclusive descriptor, but dysgraphia is the problem in school. If dyslexia is a problem of input, dysgraphia is a problem of output. The usual identifier is bad handwriting, but there is so much more to this disorder. Children with these challenges will have trouble learning to hold their pencil and their fork with a mature grip. They may be a bit clumsy with their hands and will have very poor hand-eye coordination, although they probably have good foot-eye coordination. They cannot do two different patterns with their hands: for instance, patting their head and rubbing their stomach at the same time is difficult, as will be playing the piano or guitar. A musician friend of mine is dysgraphic and cannot play the piano. Fortunately his instrument is his voice, but he can't accompany himself. He does play the clarinet well, however, because that is one note at a time.

Because writing is so difficult, dysgraphic children may consequently have trouble learning to express themselves in writing. The solution to this problem is the computer. I have serious dysgraphia and almost failed English several times. Once I acquired a typewriter and then a computer, writing became much easier for me. Remember, typing is one letter at a time: very fast if you are good at it, but one letter nonetheless.

Dyspraxia is a disorder that involves the total body. In addition to bad handwriting, other symptoms of dyspraxia include having a hard time spelling, not remembering names and faces together, and having difficulty with left and right. I know my right from my left, but if I am asked to give directions I am likely to say the incorrect direction and point correctly. Daniel Radcliffe, who plays Harry Potter, has discussed his dyspraxia in the press, pointing out that he has trouble tying his shoelaces.

Dyscalculia

This is the "dys" of math, and there are two parts to this disorder. One part involves having a poor memory for numbers. I can't remember a telephone number long enough to dial it; I have to write it down as someone tells it to me. I can't figure out the tip in a restaurant even though it is easy for me to move the decimal over one space to get the 10 percent: what I can't do without writing the numbers down is add 10 percent twice to the original sum to figure out what to leave the server. I also reverse digits in the same way some dyslexics reverse letters. Being extremely careful, counting on my fingers, repeating what I do, using a calculator, and writing down everything solves my problems.

What I don't have is the more serious part of this disorder, in which the sufferer cannot understand concepts of math. This is the child who cannot seem to understand why math is done in a certain way; who seems lost about knowing what the next step is; or who quickly forgets how to do a problem. There is no gender difference for this disorder; boys and girls are equally affected. The problem for boys is the expectation that they are supposed to be better in math than girls are, in spite of new information that indicates there shouldn't be any gender differences in math ability. So, the affected boy may lie about having done his homework or having lost his book—anything to prevent people from finding out that he doesn't understand math. There is no treatment for this disorder, but tutoring helps. For example, an older child in the neighborhood who is looking to do some community service will do nicely. Also, using real examples seems to help because this gives the child something with which to frame the problem. If a child has a hard time remembering how to calculate the area of a space, try having him measure a rug and work with him to figure out the area of that rug. He may have more success remembering the process when he has something to visualize.

Some schools understand that children with this disorder should not be expected to take advanced algebra. If your locality does not accept dyscalculia as a learning disability, you may have to become proactive in getting the school to accept this identification. If you don't succeed, take a deep breath and just accept that abstract math will be difficult for your son. He can do basic algebra, but it will require a lot of tutoring, and geometry usually is fairly easy. Practical math such as that involved in bookkeeping is an acceptable way for the child with dyscalculia to meet the math requirements in most high schools.

STRESS REACTIONS

You learned in school that the response to a life-threatening event is called "fight-or-flight." The principle is that your body gets ready to make a decision to fight the oncoming threat or to run away. In getting ready for that decision, your body, under the influence of adrenaline, increases your heart rate. As a result, your blood pressure goes up, your breathing rate increases, sugar dumps into your blood stream, blood is sent to your muscles and your brain, and your pupils dilate. Dilated pupils enable you to collect more information about what you are looking at so the picture is clearer. Your body needs to burn sugar for energy and does that more efficiently in the presence of oxygen. That's why you are breathing hard and your heart is beating fast. Your body needs the energy in your muscles so they work well and in your brain so that you can make decisions. What your body does not need is to worry about your digestion, so blood does not go there, and the body sends blood away from your skin so that if you get cut, you are less likely to bleed to death.

A child may have a physical reaction—he might yell or stand up suddenly or stomp out of a room—which can be misconstrued as purposeful when in fact it is just a normal fight-or-flight reaction to stress.

Everyone knows this is the normal way humans react to stress, but many women *do not* react this way. New information indicates that their bodies may react in a different manner in a response called "tend-and-befriend." The theory is that in order to protect those around them, women developed this "quieter appearing" response, which occurs because of the effect of oxytocin. (Experts use the term quieter appearing because women appear to shut down, and so look quieter, but inside they can be very upset.) In this reaction, blood goes to the core of the body, and the individual may be unable to move or to think; may feel sick or nauseated; may become ashy or pale and cry; and may be less visually aware of events in the surrounding because of the constriction of the pupils. The symptoms of the tend-and-befriend reaction to stress may be exacerbated by test anxiety, which appears to be more common in girls than in boys. If a child responds in this fashion, it will not help to speak sharply to or to stress her or him further. A gentle response that provides support will help this child deal with the results of reaction to stress.

In chapter 3, we discussed the rules of discipline, and #7 was not to sugarcoat the message. This is why that is important. The problem for a boy is that if those around him speak gently in an attempt not to startle him, he may not view the adult's reaction as meaningful or serious. "Honey, please clean up your room," may be seen by a boy as a suggestion. What he needs is, "Clean up your room now." And that sentence needs to be somewhat firm so the boy understands that the adult means what he or she is saying. That direct approach is not yelling and it is not being mean; it is simply factoring in the way boys process information.

COMPETITIVENESS

We already discussed the forms competitiveness can take, but when your son reaches elementary school age, you are going to see his competitiveness blossom, primarily because he is being compared to other children on a daily basis. The conversation of boys is peppered with statements like: "I bet I can do it better/ faster than you." Or "I finished my worksheet first." They will compete in matters of physical prowess, grossness (I'm not giving examples; if you are the parent of a boy, you know what I am talking about), obscure facts about sports teams, or ability on their favorite computer game, but boys rarely compete in academics. It is partially an example of that pragmatism they are known for: boys won't compete when they know they can't win. This is also partially an example of their lack of interest in school, and partially their conviction that you succeed in school because of ability, not effort.

Why boys have this idea about ability vs. effort we have no idea, because most girls tend to think the exact opposite, namely, that success is based on effort not ability. Boys certainly know that effort pays off in sports, but if you listen to them, you will realize that they know that even if someone works hard to improve at a sport, if they don't have the underlying ability, they will never truly succeed. By the way, boys don't really mind losing. What they don't like is being told that "everyone is really a winner." They know that isn't true, and it cheapens the win for those who truly do succeed at any endeavor. So, do everything you can to prevent participation trophies. Giving each child on a team something to indicate he is a winner because he participated in a losing effort tells a boy in no uncertain terms that he is a loser. Not only is he a loser; you must think he cannot possibly ever win no matter how hard he tries because why else would you have given him such a mark of his failure.

What participation trophies actually do is reduce a boy's self-esteem and his confidence. Participation trophies are any form of award given to those who did not win. They are usually given to all the members of the losing team, not select individuals who played. The idea seems to be that each child tried hard and should be recognized for his effort. This is a terrible idea for several reasons.

- Boys are competitive. They want to WIN. Giving someone a trophy for losing seems absurd to them. If everyone gets an award, there is no incentive to win, so they may give up.
- Boys are competitive. They know that losing is part of winning. If someone wins, someone else has to lose, but that isn't permanent. Next time they could be the winner. Participation trophies make it seem as if losing is okay, and they know it is not.

- Boys know that losing a game or a tournament does not label you as a loser—not forever, at least. As long as you practice and try hard, there is always hope.

Those who like the idea of participation trophies have told me they don't want their sons to be disappointed and hurt by losing. They see and hear their sons coming back from a losing effort yelling that the officiating was unfair and that the other team cheated. These parents just want to make their sons feel better by recognizing their efforts in the game. What these parents do not understand, though, is that losing only drives a boy to work harder. The more he develops animosity toward another team, the more he cares about the outcome, and the harder he will try to overcome the enemy. Sound like fighting a war? Absolutely! And no one gives participation trophies for losing a war.

It is losing that helps a boy learn to become a winner. If children win all the time, they don't value winning, and they don't understand the effort required to win. Then, when they do lose, they simply give up. Boys need the challenge to motivate themselves; otherwise, they just let others carry the load.

The Concept of fairness

For boys, the concept of fairness involves following the rules. If someone wins because they cheated, that's not fair. On the other hand, if you lose because the other guy was better than you, that is fair. For girls, the concept of fairness seems to involve evenness. If you and I hold the same job, we should get the same pay even though you do the job better. People who think this way believe that effort should be recognized and rewarded even when the work is not as good. I am always surprised at my students who think that putting a pretty cover on their work is going to get me to look more favorably on the paper because it indicates that they tried harder.

What you want is for your son to try his hardest. Boys have no trouble doing this in sports. Haven't you known them to spend hours shooting baskets or dribbling a soccer ball to improve their technique? However, they won't spend the same sort of time on writing to improve their skills or reading to improve their knowledge. The point is that improvement in physical skills is clear to a boy: you can score more points this week than you could last week. Improvement in academic skills is much less obvious to him, partially because studying may not make a difference until a month or six weeks into the future, and partially because he's experienced studying one set of facts and still not doing well as a result of lacking other skills. For example, no matter how hard I tried to learn my spelling words, I rarely got all the words correct. Now I know that one of the problems of dysgraphia is poor spelling. On the other hand, I could ace a vocabulary test every time as long as the teacher didn't take off for my poor spelling. Don't be discouraged—either one of you. Start early with your son and the early effort will pay off. Make a skill chart and each several days mark how many letters of the alphabet he knows or how many multiplication facts he has memorized.

Most boys begin playing on a sport's team when they are in elementary school. Participating in sports at this stage is for the benefits of getting exercise, working with others, and developing social skills, not aiming to be a future sports star. When a coach singles out a player as either the reason for the team's success or the team's failure, that does not encourage group feeling. (Selecting one team member as the most valuable player is not the same thing, however, especially if that individual is the most valuable for being a team player.) If the focus of your son's team is on winning, find another team. For recreation-level sports, the emphasis should be on cooperative competition—it's all about the team—and skill building, not in accumulating trophies.

There is one exception to this. If your son has truly outstanding skills, he will need a team that plays at his competitive level, but only if he has the interest. Just because your son has the skills does not mean he cares that much about the sport. The child who loves the activity will practice it on his own. It is not playing that motivates this child, it is developing his skills, and he competes primarily with himself to do better. This is the boy who will spend hours alone practicing various ways to kick or throw the ball. When a talented child does not want to compete and is pushed to do so by his parents, the result is usually not good. This is mainly because the child will not try as hard as he could. Any coach will tell you he or she would rather have a mediocre player with lots of determination than a superior player who doesn't care. Watch your son to see what he does on his own then find an activity that matches.

Outside of School

As your son grows up, what he learns inside of school and what he is experiencing outside of school begin to link up. Games are a classic example. Sometimes it seems as if boys are totally absorbed with playing games. And, for that matter, it doesn't seem to change when they grow up. Many men even refer to their careers using game terms: "That's a slam dunk" (in reference to a sure thing); "I want you on my team" (when hiring someone); "The ball's in your court" (when it is now the other person's responsibility). In fact, if you are interested in more of them there are numerous websites devoted to business-related sports clichés.

The problem is that if you don't play games with your son, he won't learn how to conduct himself the way you want him to.

Playing Go Fish with your family is one of the best ways to learn to become a grateful winner and a gracious loser. After all, you have to live with your opponents, and they are not likely to let you gloat or sulk for long. Playing lots of games also puts winning and losing in perspective. Losing a soccer game when you are eight isn't such a crushing blow if you are the Gin Rummy champion of your family; you know you can win at something.

Let's take a look at the various types of games you can encourage your son to play at this stage in his development. Remember, sometimes a game that he first plays while a grade-schooler can turn into a lifelong hobby.

STRATEGY GAMES

The most popular strategy game with boys is chess. The origins of chess are plainly military, and most chess pieces are dressed in armor or other military gear. The moves of the game are not hard to learn, and anyone can have a challenging game with another player of similar skill. This game requires players to plan long in advance for moves that may get foiled by the other player. During chess the game plan frequently needs to be reevaluated, which teaches impulse control and delay of gratification, both lessons all children—particularly boys—need to learn. Do not give your child a computer chess game, however. The whole point of chess is to pit your skills against another person's. One way that parents and children can play a game is for each player to make only one move a day. You both might find this frustrating, but it really teaches you to think over moves and to control impulses. If you can't play chess, learn the game along with your child. Most recreation centers have chess classes. Start boys in chess when they are around six to eight years old.

Checkers is a simpler form of chess and thus a good place to start. It is much quicker to play, so it's the game of choice when you want a strategy game but don't have a lot of time. Chinese checkers is a bit more complicated, especially when you have six people playing, but the problem with this strategy game is the marbles. If the board gets jostled, there is no way to remember the original locations of all of the pieces! Nevertheless, it's a great game. Start boys in checkers when they are around four to six years old.

Another game in this class is the game of bridge. (Although it belongs under the next heading, "Card Games," its strategic value trumps that category.) Bridge seems to be fading in interest because it is complicated and takes some skill. Spades or Hearts are variants, which are a bit simpler and thus a good place to start. The bidding nature of bridge requires individuals to put together small bits of information to determine what the opponents have in their hands and what is the best you can do with your cards without actually seeing anyone else's cards. The advantage for bridge is that it is intensely competitive, and it requires thinking ahead and working in concert with another person—all skills that all children need to acquire. Spades and Hearts can be learned when boys are around 7 or 8 and Bridge when they are around 10 or 12.

CARD GAMES

Poker seems to be the most popular card game at the moment, and it has the advantage of following simple rules. But don't be fooled. Skill at poker requires good interpersonal skills to figure out what your opponents are thinking, as well as sharp mathematical skills. Gambling is something that boys like because of the risk involved. Families have been known to play poker with chips, but instead of cashing them in for money, the winner gets excused from his most onerous family job for one day only. (The loser has to take it on for him.) As long as the members of the family are evenly matched, this works well. However, if younger members are more often the losers, teach your children what handicapping is all about. Develop a system so that the same winners do not always get the advantage. Simpler forms of poker can be learned starting from age eight.

Go Fish, Old Maid, Crazy Eights, and War for young children; Rummy and its variants, Canasta, Cribbage, and Spit for older children; all are played with a regular deck of cards. If you are not sure how to play these games, there are several places on the Internet that supply the rules. Teach your child how to play several different variations of solitaire with cards. If he points out that he can play on a computer, reply that he may not always be in a place with a computer, although he may find that difficult to comprehend. More importantly, playing with a real deck develops thinking skills that won't happen on the computer because its programs remember everything, such as to turn over three cards at once.

Play card games because it's more about the conversation and interaction among the players than the game itself. Families with regular "card nights" will find their children bringing their friends home to join in rather than going out with them to places you are not necessarily comfortable with. Children who are as young as three can play go fish if they recognize numbers.

BOARD GAMES

For a while board games went out of style, but they have made a comeback in spite of the popularity of computer games. If you are not familiar with board games, start with the classics: Candy Land or Chutes and Ladders, Monopoly, Clue, Rook, Risk; the list goes on. These are simply some of the ones that have been around for a long time. If your favorite game isn't listed here, remember there is no way I could possibly list them all. Candy Land and Chutes and Ladders can be played from age three and up.

Board games that do not require any language but use number recognition are Parcheesi, Backgammon, and Dominos. These are excellent games for young children to help them make the transition from games of luck, like Candy Land, to games of skill.

Board games that require knowledge or spelling include Boggle,

Scrabble, or Trivial Pursuit. Boys may like the spelling games less than the knowledge games, but this is a great place for them to actually acquire some spelling skills. On the other hand, you may be surprised to note how much your son likes showing off his knowledge of facts about certain categories.

Respect for the rules

All families have "house rules" for acceptable behavior as well as for playing various games. Your children need to understand that those rules may not be the standard. For example, if at your house the youngest player starts the game in Go Fish, make sure you tell your children that not everyone has the same rules. If a friend joins the family game, that is an excellent time to mention the family rules, and you might ask the friend to describe his family's rules and offer to play the game that way for a change. The rules for most games are available on the Internet, although you may find that not every source totally agrees. However, such information can serve to settle disputes.

What children should learn is that rules exist for a reason. Of course, one reason for the rules is that they make the game what it is, but they also exist to make the game fair for everyone. If we all play using the same set of rules, then only luck in games of chance or skill in more complicated games makes the difference. Changing the rules to suit the player means you are not playing the game. On the other hand, developing an alternate version of a game is one of the reasons why there are so many different forms of solitaire.

Following the stated rules is one of the best ways for children to learn to get along with others. If they insist on playing their own way, they will find that others may not be so charitable and refuse to let them play. Learning to get along with others is partially a matter of playing by the rules. He who cheats is usually not asked to join in again.

PHYSICAL GAMES

Tag and its variants, such as Hide and Seek, Sardines, Red Rover and Marco Polo (usually played in a swimming pool), are excellent ways to get your child moving. These are also great ways for children to learn that being knocked down is not the end of the world and that tagging someone does not require much more than a tap. Statues and Simon Says are more controlled versions of tag in which the touch is made verbally—"Freeze!" and "You moved, and I didn't say Simon Says." Playing these games with everyone in the neighborhood in the early evening during the summer is the stuff memories are made of.

Give your son the chance to play games with balls that do not involve an established team. It is astounding how much fun boys can have playing the basketball version of "Horse" in someone's driveway. If you don't know the rules of this game, any boy with a basketball hoop can enlighten you. You will find that oftentimes boys will make up games, which are determined by the equipment, location, and number of players available. These are the best games because the boys are using their own imaginations and negotiating the rules themselves.

Many parents will want to step in when they see that their child is losing. DON'T. It is essential for adults to *stay out of the physical games.* Aside from the fact that you either have an unfair advantage if the children are young or they have an unfair advantage as they grow up, it is their game, not yours. (By the way, any decision you make will not solve the problem, nor will it suit any of the combatants.) The point of neighborhood games is to help children learn to negotiate disputes rather than turning to adults to solve their problems. Remember, no matter how much you want to do so

You cannot fight your child's battles!

By stepping in, your child will now be identified as a loser. From that point on, the rest of the kids will put the universal sign for a loser (bringing the thumb and forefinger of their right hand up to their forehead, which makes an L) when they see him.

The only way we all learn to defend ourselves is to actually stand up for ourselves. This takes practice. I know you don't want to see your child upset and angry, but it won't last, I promise. The more success he has in standing up for himself, the more self-confidence he will gain. By stepping in, you actually undermine your child's confidence and his self-esteem will drop because he thinks you don't believe he can fight his own battles. It is better to teach your child how to deal with bullies, which includes staying out of their way. This does not mean you cannot step in if the 16-year-old neighborhood bully steals your 8-year-old son's basketball and pushes him in the bushes as he does so. The reason you should step in here is the age difference: an 8-year-old is too little to stand up to a teenager. If your son is close to home, he gets you to help; if he is away from home, he should look for an adult to help him.

COMPETITION

As you've seen and just read to confirm, you don't have to teach boys about competition: they come into the world with that already programmed and will bet on which water drop will get to the bottom of the window first. Girls can be just as competitive, but for them it tends to be more personal than it is with boys. Yes, boys compete with each other, and it can be very personal, but they are less likely to take either failure or success as defining them unless an adult encourages them to do so—so don't do that.

How might you actually be encouraging your son to see success or failure as defining him? You might be saying things like, "Wow, you are the best." Or "It wasn't your fault you guys lost; it was the ref." What should you say instead? "Your skills are really improving. I could tell you've worked on that shot." Or "Sorry you guys lost. The other team was good, but with a bit of practice, you should be able to take them."

See the difference? The defining approach says that skills are what they are; working harder isn't going to improve them. The major problem with this approach is that if a child fails, he doesn't understand he hasn't *totally* failed. He sees his success as global and he has no remedy to fix his problems. When you focus on specific skills, a boy can see that he has both strengths and weaknesses and he is able to work hard to improve in the areas that need some attention. This child doesn't take failure as a global assessment of himself; he knows it is due to only one or two skills that he can do something about or he can decide to change his focus altogether.

Play for real

I'm always surprised when parents brag about letting their child win. If the child will have no chance of winning then the game is too advanced for the child to play with an adult. If the child has a chance then letting him win does not teach him how to play. Also, children come to expect to win all the time, and—quite rightly—they get upset when they lose. It appears as if parents let children win based on the mistaken impression that if a child loses to an adult that boy or girl will lose self-confidence. Children expect to lose to adults, however, and when they find out they won only because the adult let them, that's when they lose self-confidence. Here's how a child thinks: "That adult is letting me win. He/She doesn't think I am capable of winning. So, I'm not even going to try."

The other reason not to let children win is that it sets up unrealistic expectations in them. When they begin to play with people outside of their families, they will expect to continue to win. When they don't, they either get angry because they think that other people are not playing fair or they get depressed because they think they are no good.

Besides, letting children win is a form of cheating, and you don't want your child to think that is acceptable behavior. Honesty in all things means that you deal fairly with everyone. There really is no difference between cheating to win or cheating to lose.

Make sure that the game is fair for the level of your child. And you might want to consider giving a child an older partner to play with. The partner can help the child learn to read the cards or the spots on the dice and to make decisions. (For instance, a youngster might need help realizing that when he is asked for all of his kings in Go Fish and he has three of them, he has to hand them all over.) At no point, however, does the partner take over.

Constructive competition

When they compete constructively, children use the competition to make themselves better, not to beat themselves up. In playing games with your children, you have the chance to model how to win and lose. More importantly, your child can learn that failure isn't the worst thing; the worst thing is failing to even try because it is a guarantee of losing.

Direct competition

A head-to-head contest with someone else is direct competition. This is the type of contest that we think of when we say that boys are competitive. The world already encourages boys to engage in this sort of competition, so they don't need you to pile on. Don't try to downplay this either, though; if you try, your son will think you do not understand him. The most important lesson you can teach your child here is that winning is not everything. Neither is it the only thing, as Vince Lombardi once said. Winning is important, but failure does not mean total failure; it only means failure in this one endeavor. (Don't forget, Lombardi was only interested in football.) Winning and losing are steps along the way toward understanding ourselves. It's about the process. I don't think your eight-year-old will understand that totally, but say things like, "I know that hurts, but there is always a next time." Or "It's frustrating to try and not succeed, but you really have made progress."

Indirect competition

Competing with yourself, your own performance record, is indirect competition. It's what we think of in sports as getting a "personal best." Boys see this very clearly in athletics and will spend all afternoon trying to perfect a jump shot. As you've heard me ask before, why won't that same child spend half an hour reviewing his spelling words? Part of the issue is that in sports the skills are defined and progress is clearly visible. In academics, the definition of success keeps changing. In sports, if you score more points, you win. In academics, learning how to solve math problems just means that you get more complicated math problems handed to you.

I believe there's one more factor to consider here. Adults downplay failures because they are concerned that a child not be hurt by the bruised ego that comes with losing. They either make the task easier or the task count less. Children, as I've explained, see that as evidence the adults think they are not very smart. But consider this. In sports, if you can't slam-dunk, you don't get to lower the rim; you simply have to work harder or wait until you are a little taller. What parents can do for their sons is to help them learn to identify areas where they are good and where they have trouble, and work with them to ameliorate the trouble spots. Charts can help a child see his progress. You don't need to provide a payoff such as stickers or other prizes; setting a personal best is prize enough. Besides, if you reward success in a tangible way, your son will learn to work only for that prize and not for the good feeling that success brings. As your child gets older, you may be tempted to pay him for grades. We will discuss that in the next chapter.

Cooperative competition

When boys compete as part of a group working for a common goal, it's called cooperative competition. All of the group exercises your son will do in school are designed to help him learn to work as part of the team. Again, this is clearer in sports. If you don't pull your weight and don't practice, it is obvious to everyone. In a school project, the student who spends the most time talking about the project and telling everyone how great it is may be the student who is doing the least work. The problem with cooperative competition comes sometimes in figuring out just how much each member of the group contributes to the final product.

Games Are Important

Playing games is serious and school-age children need to be totally involved in their games. What do children gain by playing games?

- They learn that the rules are the rules and you can't change them, in the same way that 2+2 always equals 4.

THE PARENTS' GUIDE TO BOYS

- They learn that unless you really try, you don't accomplish much. Playing for fun may pass the time, but you don't improve your skills that way.
- They learn to work with others and to be a productive part of a group effort. They'll see that divisiveness on a team will guarantee unsatisfactory results.
- They learn to trust others and to be trustworthy. They'll see that if someone makes promises and does not follow through, everyone loses.

Suggestions from the Teacher

The elementary school child needs to acquire lots of life skills. If you can help your son in the following areas, he will have a distinct advantage in class.

HANDSHAKES

When your son enters elementary school, he is old enough to be introduced to others as his own man, so to speak. This means he should know how to shake the hand of another person and begin to learn the proper etiquette of handshakes. In business, some of these rules no longer are observed, but until he is in that position, he should follow these guidelines:

- He does not offer his hand to an older person until he is much older; he waits until the more senior person offers his hand to him. There are ways he can signal that he is willing to shake hands, though, and you can share some of your secrets with him on how to do that.

- He always waits for a woman to offer her hand to him, no matter what her age is.
- He looks in the eyes of the person whose hand he is shaking and either repeats his or her name or acknowledges that person in some way. Some boys find it difficult to look in another person's eyes; in this case, if he will look at the man's or woman's forehead or between the eyebrows, it will appear as if he is looking in the other's eyes.
- He has a firm grip, but not too firm. (By the way, boys love practicing shaking hands.)

TAKE YOUR SON OUT

When teachers take children on field trips, one of the major issues is the boys and girls who don't know how to stand in line, how to be quiet where appropriate, and how to listen for directions. It isn't that much different from what they are required to do in school, but being in the different venue seems to mean to them that the rules are different.

So please take your child to the movies and teach him not to talk out loud during the movie. It's not the same as watching at home. Take your child to museums and teach him how to look at exhibits and how to listen to what a docent is saying about what he's looking at. Make sure that your first visits are appropriate for children: for example, they like exhibits about Egypt but not necessarily fine art. I took my son to the National Gallery in Washington when he was about 10, and he was not interested until we got to a special exhibit of Claes Oldenburg's work. You know his sculpture—an enormous typewriter eraser and the equally enormous clothespin. My son was tickled at the puns and humor evident in Oldenburg's art and he remains a favorite today. Take your son to see *The Nutcracker* at Christmas; it's a festive way to introduce him to ballet. If you know of a children's concert, make sure that your son attends. Be a good role model and stand in line quietly and patiently and encourage your son to do the same.

Be careful when you take your son out to a restaurant; both the food and the location should be appropriate for your son's tastes and energy level. When my son was very little, for instance, my husband belonged to a service club that met one night a week for dinner. I would often take my son out to eat on those nights because the restaurants were typically not crowded on a weeknight, and since it was just the two of us, he had my full attention. He learned early how to sit at a table, how to order, and what to expect about how and when the food was served. By the time he was six, he was a pleasure to go out to dinner with, even if we weren't going to fine tablecloth restaurants.

You'll benefit from teaching your son how to behave in public, and your son's teachers will also appreciate your efforts in this area.

MONEY

As you take your older child shopping with you, plan carefully so that you spend as little time as possible in the stores and engage your child in conversation teaching him about the items. My mother talked all the time while she was shopping telling me what was going on in her mind and I did the same with my son. "We need to get some sheets for your big-boy bed. It is a twin bed. See here on the package where the size is? Yes, those sheets are fun, but let's see how they feel. They seem a bit scratchy. Do you think you might be happier with softer sheets? What about these?" These are conversations similar to the ones that we had before he could talk only now, I was actually trying to teach him what was going on in my head as we went through a store. My son learned about how to shop and learned what to look for. That conversation was a good example of the difference between want and need.

Giving your child *things* is not the way to win their affection. The only item you can give your child that he really wants is your presence. That matters more to children than anything you can buy. Spend time with your child, not money on him. I know your child will tell you that *everyone* he knows has that particular brand of shoe or video game. It isn't true and what your child really wants is for you to listen to him and acknowledge that you understand what he is talking about. Ask him what makes the item so great, why is it better than another similar item, what could he do to earn the money for the item. Giving children something actually distances them from you.

My cousin traveled a lot for his job, and instead of bringing home useless toys, he would leave a bit of money wherever he went—nothing much, a penny usually. When he got home, he would talk about where he had been, and the game was for the children to guess where he had put the penny. That made them feel that they had been with him on his trip. I don't think that the children ever found the pennies, but they knew that their father had been thinking of them while on his trip. These days you could take a picture with a cell phone of the penny and send it to your son. Even more evidence of you thinking of him.

You do need to help your child learn to manage his money. Help your child see the connection between having money and spending money. When he is in elementary school, his allowance should be just enough for him to buy items you won't buy for him: gum, candy, comic books, and the like. Don't let him slip those items into the basket on the theory that you will pay for them. If he has an allowance, then he pays for those items. That may sound harsh, but if you start that way, he will never expect you to cover his incidental expenses. The sooner he makes that connection, the less likely he will be to splurge on unnecessary items and come begging for money from you. As the old folks say, start as you mean to go on.

INDEPENDENCE

When I was little, the only games we played where adults were involved were when teachers supervised our PE classes. We played soccer and baseball in school, and the better students played on a school team that competed with other schools. On weekends, the rest of us played games we made up. I'm always amused by readers' interest in "Calvin Ball," the game made up by the boy in the comic strip *Calvin and Hobbes*. The game changed all the time—and that was the point! When we weren't playing officially recognized games, we were playing games together in nonstructured ways. There weren't adults around to enforce the rules or to tell us that we had the rules wrong. We made it up as we went along.

One of the concerns about children in the 21st century is that many of them never play without adult direction. They play ball games, but only in organized leagues with adult coaches. They play computer games, but those were written by adults. They are not allowed to be out of sight of adults.

I know that parents are terrified their child will get hurt. But new research indicates that children get hurt more often on engineered playground equipment than they do in vacant lots. One possible reason for this is that because everything seems so safe, children and parents let down their guard. Another problem arises because playground equipment is so safe it's boring, so children start to do things with the equipment that are not what the designer intended.

And that's when kids get hurt. Children want some level of risk in their lives, and safe playgrounds don't offer that.

Another concern is that if children are on their own, they are at risk of being abducted. The national statistics on missing children are an indicator of how serious this problem is. However, the number of children taken by strangers is very small. The data for this is very hard to extract, but at the best guess, your child is only slightly less likely to die playing high school sports than to be taken by a stranger and not returned voluntarily. The overwhelming number of individuals who take children are either family members or people well known to the family. The National Incidence Studies of Missing, Abducted, Runaway, and Thrownaway Children for 2002 estimates that of the 797,000 children taken that year 115 were "stereotypical" kidnapping, namely, children taken by a stranger or someone of slight acquaintance at least for an overnight period, and 57 percent of those incidents ended with the return of the child. The most common reason why children went missing was that they either ran away from home or they were thrown away by parents (that is, told to leave home or prevented from returning home).

All children need time to be independent of authority figures. Children who live in the suburbs or in the country have space and places in which to play, but children in the city have far less open space available to them. So if you live in the city encourage your child to get involved in unstructured activities such as indoor climbing, laser tag, or paint ball. Skateboards are very popular, but make sure that your child wears appropriate padding at the beginning. As he becomes surer of himself, he won't want to wear the padding, but point out that the pros wear helmets, gloves, and long pants. Yes, he is likely to get hurt, but keeping him from injury means that he never experiences anything. As I've mentioned before, risk is key for boys. You have the choice between letting him fall out of a tree and breaking his arm at 6 or driving a car into a tree and risking his life when he is 16.

Why is this so important?

Imagination can build only when an individual's thoughts aren't directed by anyone. I realized that when the first *Harry Potter* movie came out. It was the first movie in a long time where the kids had read the book before they saw the movie. As we were exiting the very crowded theater, I overheard two boys, probably around 10 years old, discussing the movie. One pointed out that the movie had the game "Quidditch" all wrong, and his friend agreed. The first boy began to describe how the game was really played, and the other looked shocked. "That's not how it goes!" he said. The point was that each boy had built a mental picture of the game and the pictures did not match. Each boy's imagination had constructed the game differently. Children who just see movies and play only league soccer never have a place in which to develop their imagination. Everything they do and see is interpreted by an adult.

Nature is foreign territory to many children. They have never been in woods, meadows, or creeks; they have never climbed a tree; they have never hiked or climbed a mountain; they have never paddled a canoe in a wilderness area; they may never have been to a state or national nature preserve or park. The only time many children go outside is to walk from a vehicle to a building and back again; to ride in the vehicle to go to an amusement park, swim in a community or backyard pool, or play a sport on an athletic field. A lot of schools don't have recess anymore because it is "wasted time."

Certainly, one reason to get children outdoors is to have them exercise. Given the problem with childhood obesity, this is an obvious factor. The real reason for children to interface with nature, however, is that it is so unpredictable. Playing games that are adult-structured means that the experience is predictable. Go to your local swimming pool, it looks the same year after year. Go to your local swimming hole, it may change from day to day depending on rainfall and other local conditions. Nature requires your attention. You can walk down a sidewalk without looking at your feet, but you can't walk down a path without watching carefully or you are likely to trip on a rock. I'm always fascinated by the children I meet who are totally oblivious to what is going on around them. Without some understanding of nature, we do not appreciate our effect on the world around us, yet with the acceleration of environmental problems, that knowledge is crucial to survival.

If you don't pay attention to those around you, you miss out on a lot of what is going on. And being prepared for life means that you can deal with the random nature of the world and are able to cope with what happens. Acquiring the skills to cope with life can only happen when you engage in life as it really happens. It may look as if kids are wasting their time when they are goofing off, but they are actually learning how to manage what happens to them. Don't interfere.

Boredom is something children complain of, and many will turn to their parents to amuse them. Few children know how to entertain themselves. On the other hand, many children believe that something with electricity is required for entertainment: TV, computer, and amusement parks leap to mind. Children who are given the outdoors as a playground can always find something to do even if it is just digging a hole in the backyard to make mud to slide in.

When your children complain that there is nothing to do and they are bored, send them outside. You might want to take them to a park, but most of all, don't feel responsible to entertain them. Children will learn early how to amuse themselves if you let them. Just give them lots of toys without batteries, such as blocks, cars, balls, swings, all the classics. Or when your child complains of boredom, offer to entertain him with household chores. *That's* a surefire way to get him out of your hair. Remember, it's not up to you to entertain him when he is young, and don't let him park himself in front of the TV or he will never learn to entertain himself.

I was amused when we took our six-year-old son to visit friends who lived in the city. At home, he had a backyard and woods to play in, building forts, watching bugs, catching snakes, digging holes, and a host of invented games. At the friends' house, there was a neat backyard with a play structure. Once he had swung and gone down the slide for about half an hour, he came to me complaining that there was nothing for him to do. The friend suggested that he watch TV, but he pointed out that he was only allowed an hour of TV a day during vacation and there wasn't anything on that he wanted to see. He wasn't a good reader at the time so that wasn't an option. Eventually, I found a deck of cards and showed him how to build structures with them. As an adult, my son has many activities that interest him, but he has pointed out that many of his friends seem to be interested only in watching sports. Our son was raised to be self-sufficient and doesn't need others to entertain him today.

GROUPS SEEM MORE IMPORTANT THAN FAMILY

Once your son gets to elementary school, you will find that his friends seem more important to him than does his family. Absolutely true. Research has discovered that boys get more social support from their male peers than from their parents and even from girl friends. It is the group to which he belongs that will define your son more than his membership in your family. He is a "geek" or a "jock" not a "Smith" or a "Jones." I promise you that at some point you will want to say to your boy, "If your friends told you to jump off a mountain, you'd do it!"

Don't despair. In the long run, your son knows that his family is always there, but for boys, family is not enough. They need their group, too, which is probably why boys enjoy being on sports teams and belonging to skateboarding groups. Encourage your son to bring his friends home, provide food, tolerate the noise, and give them an acceptable place to play. Do not let them park in front of the TV or computer; persuade them to engage in activities. Take them to the skate park, the science museum, or any place they can get out and run.

What do you do for the boy who does not seem to have any friends? There are a number of reasons for this, and it will help if you and your son explore the reasons together.

1. Some boys are shy and find it difficult to interact with others. This child will be well served by getting involved in a structured activity that he likes, such as being part of a rocketry team or a musical group. Make sure that whatever he does is with other children, although there should be no pressure for him to engage with the other children, just work with them.

2. Some boys have interests that are unusual, such as dance or science activities. If you live in an urban or suburban area, you can generally find a group for your son to belong to. You may have to drive a bit, but the group is there. If you live in a more rural area this can be a problem. Specialty summer camps will help, and contacts made there may help your son find a group of friends.

3. Some boys have poor social skills. It can be very hard to admit that your child does not make friends easily, so if you are not sure why your child does not have a group to which to belong, ask his teacher or someone else at his school. If poor social skills are mentioned, there are programs to help children develop these skills, and I urge you to enroll your child.

4. Sometimes there just don't seem to be other children that your child gets along with, and that can be very hard because there is nothing particular to "fix." One of my former students told me that he did not have any close friends in elementary school or high school and he worried about that. It was not until he got to college that he found his group. At that point, he discovered that when he was younger his dry sense of humor was seen as negative, but his humor was viewed as an asset as his peers matured. He said that his parents were very supportive of anything that he tried and that was very helpful to him.

CHORES

By the time children are in school, you can expect them to be responsible for feeding pets, emptying trash cans, sorting laundry, and putting groceries away. A third grader can make his lunch (with some supervision), weed flower beds, walk a moderately sized dog, fold clean laundry, clean the bathtub he has just used, and sweep. A fifth grader can do the laundry, mow the lawn (as long as you don't have a lot of hills in your lawn; moving a mower up and down hills takes strength), run the vacuum cleaner, and clean the entire bathroom.

Watch carefully when your child begins a new chore to make sure that he can do it properly. A full garbage can is heavy compared to a wastepaper basket, for example, so a younger child can be responsible for trash long before he can lift the garbage can.

Your child also needs to learn to troubleshoot. If he leaves the garbage outside the back door and does not take it to the trash can because that is too far away, he has to deal with the mess the next morning made by dogs or other animals that got into the bags and strewed the contents all over the neighborhood. He can ask for your help, but he is in charge. It is his responsibility to get someone to do his chores when he goes to a friend's house for a sleepover. If he fails to do so, he will be required to do someone else's chores in addition to his own for several days.

Likewise, if your child fails to make his lunch, he goes to school without one. He won't starve, I promise. If he fails to take out the garbage, you can refuse to do some chore that affects him until he does his job.

What do you want your child in elementary school to be able to do?

- Expand his reading skills, or at least enjoy being read to.
- Begin the process of learning self-control and self-motivation
- Be able to entertain himself.
- Develop responsibility through chores and following through on obligations.
- Start learning to become independent.

CHAPTER 5

BUILDING A BENIGN DICTATORSHIP (YOU'RE THE DICTATOR): MIDDLE SCHOOL

Opportunity is missed by most because it is dressed in overalls and looks like work. —Thomas Alva Edison

If you're not failing every now and again, it's a sure sign that you're not trying anything innovative. —Woody Allen

Middle school is hard for everyone because there is so much going on. In elementary school, students are children. In high school, students are adolescents. In middle school, some students (mostly boys) are children and some students (mostly girls) are adolescents. Hormones drive almost every student to one extent or another. Some teachers enjoy this hodgepodge of students, abilities, interests, developmental levels, and physical maturities, and you should be very grateful when your child is taught by one of these people.

Children in elementary schools think in terms of real events. They love projects because that gives them physical tasks to complete and check off a list. As children go through puberty, they begin to be able to deal in concepts and can think in terms of "what if?" In a science class at this level, some of the students will be able to understand the basics of the material and others will be able to understand the principles from that material and see how they apply to a larger concept. It can be hard for a teacher to meet the needs of the concrete thinkers who don't always understand the concepts and, at the same time, meet the needs of the abstract thinkers who may find the focus on specific examples somewhat limiting.

Research suggests there may be a difference along gender lines between abstract thinkers and concrete thinkers. Many of the girls are going to be ready to think about concepts whereas many of the boys will still be thinking about facts. This will not be true for all children, and boys who develop the abstract thinking skills early will probably have a more positive outlook about school because they are getting the point of what the teacher is trying to get them to learn. Students who continue to focus on memorization of facts will do fine in middle school, but they will have trouble when they get to high school. The most that parents can do to help their children develop more advanced thinking skills is to have conversations with them about whys rather than whats. For example, if it is an election year, family discussions about the effects of political decisions on the family will introduce this sort of thinking to children.

Another challenging issue in middle school is the difference between boys and girls in social skills. If your son is late to develop physically, he is going to feel left out of much of the social aspects of school. Help him find some others who share his interests and abilities. This can be hard when a friend he has grown up with goes through puberty a bit earlier and starts the growth spurt. That child may be more interested in sports and girls than the boy who enters puberty later. If your child is the early developer, he may feel a bit bewildered by the attentions of somewhat older students who see him as one of them. He may also have trouble in school simply because teachers tend to respond to a child's developmental level, not to his age.

One of my students was a very smart 13-year-old high school freshman who was well over six feet tall. He got into a lot of trouble at school, and when I pointed out that most teachers

THE PARENTS' GUIDE TO BOYS

would have no trouble with his antics if he were in the eighth grade, one teacher agreed, but stated that the teen was a bit old to be an eighth grader. When I said this boy was actually the same age as most eighth graders, the teacher was astonished. She was responding to the boy's physical development, not his cognitive development—a common mistake and misconception. Children who are either earlier or later than most to develop are usually the ones who have the most trouble in middle school. If your child is one of these, make sure that the teachers are aware of your child's chronological age.

Brain Changes

The causes of the sudden changes in physical development that come with puberty are certainly connected to the sudden emotional swings that your child may exhibit now. Some children will be very emotional and others will go through puberty relatively easily. The brain continues to develop during this period and is certainly influenced by the hormones, but it is very hard to point out exactly what those influences are.

VERBAL SKILLS

I know it seems as if I am harping on this subject, but the developmental differences between boys and girls in verbal skills are a major issue in school, including middle school. Think about how hard it would be to go to school if you didn't speak or read the language that was used in class. It can seem almost that bad to late-developing boys who are baffled by their classmates' facility with understanding and producing words.

For some time, your son's verbal skills have been improving. He may not be the chattiest individual with adults, but he has made great strides, and you may be aware that he and his buddies are very talkative with each other. At the beginning of elementary school, boys are still noticeably behind girls in verbal skills, but by the end, they should have made up a great deal of the difference. However, many struggle with developing facility with words and can be easily overwhelmed by the more fluent students.

Many of the middle school boys I have taught in study skills classes have been very concerned by their slow-developing verbal skills. The mere thought of writing anything sends some of them into tailspins. Some boys, of course, are very good writers, but that tends to be the exception, not the rule. On the other hand, I have observed that boys who attend single-gender classes in middle school frequently don't have that fear because they are not comparing themselves to the more verbally confident girls.

By the end of middle school, many boys will be able to keep up with most of the girls. It is the boy who is developmentally behind the majority of his classmates who will be in real trouble. If something is not done now or soon, he may be in the group at risk for having difficulty in completing high school.

If a single-gender program is not available for your son or you are not interested in one of these programs, several interventions are available to help you help your son become a reader.

Mentor: Find an older boy with good verbal skills who has patience and is willing to work with your son. They can practice sports together and end by opening books. If your son sees this older boy as a role model and the older boy reads, your son may find that reading is interesting to him. Also, when it's the older boy who suggests a book, your son may be more willing to try it.

Graphic novels: These may seem like comic books, but the good ones (I've offered you some suggestions in the resources list at the end of the book) are just highly illustrated novels. Be very careful when you select graphic novels. There are a great many more than there used to be, but many of them are very poorly written. *Manga,* the Japanese version of graphic novels, are not appropriate for young children. Many are quite violent and some can be a bit sexist. A few series are appropriate for children between 8 and 16, so ask your librarian or an older child who is familiar with the genre for recommendations.

One of the real reasons you don't want young children reading these books is that they open left to right instead of right to left, and they are read right page first then left. Since this is the opposite of books written in English, novice readers can be confused. Additionally, if they are translated from Japanese, they don't always read as smoothly as books originally written in English.

When you select other graphic novels, start with versions of the classics and make sure that the version you get is abridged, not revised or rewritten. What you want is a book that is the same story as the classic, using the author's original words, just shorter and with pictures. There are also excellent graphic versions of Shakespeare, and one series offers two different books with two different versions of the story: one in modern English and the other in the original language.

Paper clips: If your son finds it hard to read for a long time, get some large paper clips and clip together three or four pages all the way through the book. Tell your son he only has to read one paper clip's worth of pages at a time, but when he does so, he has to write one sentence about what he read. He should do this at least once a day and twice a day on weekends. Knowing he has to tackle just a small section at each sitting means that he may be more willing to try to read.

Read with him: Get your own copy of the book your son has been assigned and read along with him. You and he can sit together reading the book, then talk about what is going on in the story after both of you have finished the chapter. Another version of this is that he reads to you while you are doing something like cooking dinner. You used to read to him, now he can read to you.

Emotions

You will notice that your middle schooler feels in-between most of the time. Some days he is your little boy, giggling over gross jokes and happy to bake cookies with you; on other days he is a teenager, morose and uncommunicative. He is as baffled by these mood swings as you are and probably concerned that something is seriously wrong with him. When he is in one of his communicative periods, mention that you've noticed he is growing up. Share with him your own stories from when you were the same age and commiserate with him how difficult it can be to not know how you are going to feel from day to day. Don't sit down and expect to have a heart-to-heart with him. This conversation will be received best when you and he are doing something together so that he is not expected to look at you.

Shoulder-to-shoulder is the way to talk to your son about serious issues at this stage in his life. Research points out that boys of this age are not as good as girls at reading other people's emotions based on facial expressions or body language. That information may confuse him. He wants to talk to you; he just doesn't want it to seem like he wants to talk to you. Take a moment when you are working with him to clean out the garage, driving back from a game, or shooting baskets in the driveway to bring up these topics.

Don't expect him to unburden himself immediately. Open the doors to communication, but don't be surprised if he isn't immediately interested. This will take a while, and you may never be satisfied with the results. He is aware of what you are doing and grateful that you are interested enough in him to try even if he has no way to let you know that. Don't push the issue. Start with a few stories of your life at his age and know that at some point he will say something like "You have no clue what I am going through." Don't tell him that you remember what it was like to be his age; instead, tell him stories about what happened to you and what you did at his age.

One other thing I have noticed is that the concept of time for you and for your son is very different. In retrospect, the time you spent in middle school seems very short, but to your son, for whom time moves very slowly, it seems like forever. When you tell him things are going to get better shortly, you probably are thinking in terms of six months to a year. Shortly for him, on the other hand, means in the next two weeks. Be specific about time when you talk to your son at this age.

Other Developmental Hurdles

It is obvious as we watch children grow up that girls and boys do not have the same pattern of physical development. In fact, some boys may be just beginning their growth spurt at the same time when some girls are reaching their adult height. I'm particularly sensitive to this problem because I was the tallest student in my 7th grade class. The next year several of the boys had begun to overtake me, but I'm just about the same height now as I was when I was 12. On the other hand, I have known boys who were the shortest student in their 9th grade class, but by 12th grade were among the tallest in their class.

Statistics show that in any middle school classroom the child who is the last to enter puberty and to reach adult height is more likely to be a boy. In our culture, men are supposed to be taller than women; thus, for the late-developing boy, this creates all sorts of difficulties both emotional and behavioral.

Another serious issue for boys is that girls are likely to become sexually mature before their male classmates. For a boy who has been taught that masculinity depends on sexual prowess, this seems like a cruel joke. He really isn't interested in girls yet, but society says he should be. So he exaggerates his physical ability, swaggers around the girls, and is totally panicked by the notion of homosexuality because of his lack of interest in an emotional connection with girls. After all, the friend with whom he does have an emotional connection is likely to be a boy. He believes that the way he is now is the way he is always going to be, and he doesn't want anyone to know that he isn't quite the man he perceives is the cultural norm.

Consequently, boys in middle school may become bullies to cover their fear that they aren't quite as stereotypically masculine as they think the world expects them to be. They may also become interested in pornography because they really are interested in sex in general, just not specifically with a person. The advent of the Internet has made both pursuits more accessible, resulting in cyberbullying and surfing porn sites. Whatever you can do to help your son stay a little boy will help him later. This is one of the reasons why children should only access the Internet on computers in public areas such as the family room, the public library, or the schoolroom. Pushing development only results in children who think there is something wrong with them, and they start to get involved in behaviors that are too advanced (drugs, drinking, sex) or in becoming depressed because they see themselves as failures.

BULLYING

Middle school is the time when bullying activity peaks. The reason is that children are now old enough to act on their thoughts but still young enough that the part of the brain involved in self-control and making decisions based on reason is not yet fully developed. Additionally, many children of this age take behavior directed at them literally and personally. Boys tend to band together in groups of three to five to bully children they don't know very well. You can point out to your son that the bullies show their own vulnerability because they need each other for support, but that is cold comfort for the object of the attacks. Also, bullies frequently are bullied themselves and they displace their anger through harassing other children.

As you did when your son was younger, telling your preteen or teenager to ignore the bully is the correct approach, but your son won't think you have given him much help. Your son is either embarrassed or concerned about some aspect of himself, and the bully attacks him at that weak point. It is probably just chance that the bully discovers the vulnerability, but since most children in middle school are vulnerable in some way, it is just a matter of time before another child finds the chink in your son's defenses. You may want to view Lee Hirsch's documentary *The Bully Project* and then watch it with your son. You will cringe at what you see; he will likely tell you that he has seen similar events already. The reason to view this documentary is to let your son know that you are concerned and are open to discussing this problem with him.

It doesn't matter whether your son is the subject of physical, emotional, or cyber attacks; the process is the same. The group doing the bullying separates a boy from the herd, gets him isolated, and then begins to harass the boy, warning him that if he tells he will be hurt further. This is the standard approach for pretty much all forms of abuse, but your son won't know that. The process is designed to make sure that the victim does not tell anyone—particularly teachers or parents—about what is going on. So, it is quite possible your son is being bullied and neither you nor your son's teachers know about it. Children in middle school can be rather moody, and it is hard to determine whether your son is just in a sullen mood or is in distress.

One reason why bullies succeed is that the child who is the object of the attack believes that others value the bullies and that if he stands up for himself, he will lose his position in the larger group to which both the bully and the boy belong. And commonly, the child believes that the bully is right, that he really is whatever the bully says he is. Usually at this age, the attacks zero in on problems with sexual identity or lack of friendship. Because your son is convinced he is the only person who has these problems, at some level, he believes what the bullies are saying about him.

One way to address this problem is to ensure that your son's school has a good anti-bullying program in place. Make sure that you and your son are familiar with the program as well as the steps the school has in place to protect students. Unfortunately, bullying usually takes place in isolation so no adults or trained peers are around to step in and defuse the situation. The best defense for your son, therefore, is a good self-concept, some basic protection skills, and total openness with you. You need to start working with your son in those three areas before he gets to middle school.

Good Self-Concept

To help strengthen your child's self-image and self-esteem, expose your child to other children in a loosely supervised environment. Your son needs to play and work with other children his age without any interference from you. If he gets knocked down and scrapes his knee and you rush in to help, chances are the other children will see that he isn't defending himself, you are, and that means he is vulnerable. If he is able to bounce back on his own that demonstrates to him and to others that he is capable of managing himself. Children develop their self-concept through experiences, not by being told by others that they are a success. Yes, you want to help your son know what a great kid he is, but he is going to learn that lesson better through his interaction with others. He learns he is a good student because he can meet the teacher's requirements on his own, not because you help him produce perfect work.

Basic Protection Skills

It is hard to see your child get hurt and not step in, but think about what will happen in 10 years. You will not be around then to help, and the best defense you can give your boy is the knowledge that he can defend himself. That is why martial arts are so popular for children; they learn exactly how to defend themselves. That is physical defense, of course, and many of the attacks your child will come under will be emotional and psychological. Good martial arts programs include psychological defense as well, and if your son likes this sort of program, it can provide him with a great deal of self-confidence. If he can simply walk with confidence, he is less likely to be a target.

If your child is not interested in some form of physical self-defense, he needs to find an activity that will introduce him to a group of other children with similar interests. As he approaches middle school, knowing that other kids share his abilities and interests will be comforting to your son, who may otherwise think he is the only one like himself. Remember this: make sure that this is your son's interest and not something you think he would like. If he doesn't know of anything and you have exhausted all the sports available locally, consider these areas that boys typically like: drama, scouting, singing in a boys' choir, art, robotics, dancing (tap, hip hop, clogging), playing a musical instrument (a good music teacher can help him find one he likes), fort building, dirt bikes, cooking, collecting things, and bird watching, among others.

Many of these activities will require finding an adult who will either teach a skill or lead a group, but that adult should not be you. Yes, your son will be interested in video games, but that doesn't help him develop the social skills he needs to defuse personal attacks. Do not let him sink into the latest video game even if he is playing with another boy. It is fine for a while, but not for a whole afternoon.

Total Openness

Be very alert to any sign of cyber bullying either by your child or of your child. Most middle school children are not aware of the devastating effects of cruel statements on the Internet nor are they really aware that everything that is put on a computer or smart phone can be traced—forever. Make sure your child knows that. Basically, nothing should be committed to any form of electronic message that you would not be willing to shout out loud to everyone you know. If you want to know what I'm talking about, look on the Internet for embarrassing messages on social networking sites; they can be funny, but many are not what you want your child reading. Don't forget: if you can find those messages, so can your child.

The crux of middle school children's response to bullying is that they are very emotional, but don't yet have the self-confidence or self-awareness to protect themselves. They can believe everything that is said to them even when the statement is plainly sarcastic or ironic. Their bodies are beginning to grow up and you can see what they are going to look like as adults, but their emotions and thinking are more like what they have been in elementary school. Teach your child to think and act independently, with confidence, and encourage him to discuss his concerns openly with you. As a result, he will be better prepared to navigate his way around bullies in hallways or parking lots and leave them in the dust.

ADOLESCENT EGOCENTRISM

As I've referenced already in this chapter, when children enter puberty, they begin to feel as if no one else experiences things the way that they do. This phenomenon has been referred to as the *personal fable,* a term coined by David Elkind (1967). Individuals who think this way believe that their experiences are unique; as a result, no one else can possibly understand what they are going through because no one else has ever had their experiences. Pointing out to your son that you felt the same way and that his best friend does too will get you nowhere. You just don't understand. NO ONE has ever felt as he does or had to put up with all of the problems he does. His school, his friends, and—yes—his family are all against him and no one understands at all.

Another part of this is the middle school boy's belief that everyone is looking at him and focusing on his faults. Males at this age spend hours getting ready to go out and becoming fixated on what they wear or how their hair looks. True, it is common for young girls to go through this, but boys become overly concerned with their looks too. Many parent-child arguments are based on the amount of money that is required to accumulate the appropriate wardrobe or obtain the perfect acne treatment. "You don't understand!!!! I NEED this!!!!" is frequently followed by, "You don't care about me. Only my friends understand me," accompanied by the sound of a slamming door as your child retreats into his bedroom.

Which, by the way, will look like a herd of buffalo ran through it, but we will get to that a bit later.

The other side of this is that your preteen/teenager may decide he just doesn't care what other people think of him. If everyone is going to look at him let them look. He isn't going to give them the satisfaction of thinking their opinion matters to him at all. Of course, you know that he cares a great deal, but it won't help to point this out to him. The best thing you can do is continue to accept the boy you know and love no matter what the package is dressed like.

Middle school teachers are used to both versions of the personal fable. They are aware that children may be very concerned at some point with what people think of them and then do a total 180-degree turn and act as if they were not aware that anyone even noticed them. If you are concerned about the way your son is acting, talk to the teacher he respects the most and see what the teacher thinks is going on. It probably is nothing more than the usual trying on of different personalities to see which fits best, but in some cases, it can be more serious.

UNDERSTANDING OTHERS

Another part of adolescent egocentrism is that your child does not understand that others may feel differently about events than he does. Just because your 13-year-old can tell you what's going on in a TV show does not mean he experiences the events in the same way you do. You understand that what happens is the product of imagination, but even teenagers get confused between facts and fiction on the TV. (And don't get me started on "reality" TV, which isn't that either.) For example, a few of my high school students were talking about how cool and dangerous one of the shows was in which a man goes into the wilderness and deals with nature. When I pointed out that he wasn't alone—someone had to hold the camera, after all—they were shocked. That idea had never occurred to them. The egocentrism of the adolescent sometimes translates into his having a hard time understanding another's perspective.

Research indicates that in males, the right portion of the amygdala is activated to improve memory for central details; in females, the left portion of the amygdala works to improve memory for fine details. One theory is that this is the source of the different focus of females and males in emotional situations: that is, females may tend to pay attention to the basic facts and males may have a more global view of the event. This may also explain why a girl obsesses about what someone said and what she meant by those words, whereas boys are more concerned with the attitudes of those involved, but they can't remember exactly what was said.

The effect is that boys, in particular, may feel somewhat isolated from their families and from others they don't know well. Their close friends understand, mainly because they have been with them all along, but no one else seems to. Consequently, it may seem as if your son has created a new family with his group of friends.

GANGS AND GROUPS

It is common for boys to find their friends more important than their families. In elementary school, you were able to control your son's access to these friends because he was dependent on you to transport him to visit them. In middle school, your son may have wheels in the form of a bike or a skateboard, and he certainly has more freedom to get around by himself. All of a sudden, your son has friends you don't know, whose parents you don't know, and he wants to go off with them. If you don't understand this need, watch the movie *Stand by Me*, the best movie ever made about middle school boys on their own.

Not only does your son want to be off with his buddies, he needs to do that as well. And he needs to do that without adults around. This is how boys learn to work together in groups and how they start the process of learning to be responsible for others. I know you wonder why he has to do this with his friends when he has a perfectly good family to belong to. Some psychologists believe that in order for boys to grow up into manhood, they have to separate from their families. Don't forget that boys are very emotional; they don't feel comfortable all on their own, although many dream about doing that. Instead, they tend to form a new family, sort of like the Lost Boys in *Peter Pan*—boys who join together for emotional protection. We see this in many animals where young males leave the maternal group and form a band of brothers until they are ready to be adult males on their own.

What you are concerned about is that this group may be a bad influence on your son. They seem to come up with ideas you can't believe your son would have thought of on his own. Well, someone's son came up with the idea to build a bonfire in the backyard or spray paint the windows of the principal's office black, but your son is probably not going to tell you which friend is responsible. Remember, the instigator may be your boy, as hard as that is to imagine.

While this behavior is not to be condoned, it should not be thought of as delinquent either. Don't ask him, "What were you thinking?" The answer to that question is that he has no idea. He really doesn't. The idea came up and the group decided to do it without any consideration of the consequences. Middle school boys are impulsive and like taking risks. The important point is whether or not the intention was to hurt anyone. As long as there was no idea of actually hurting anyone or anything, then the whole reason for the behavior was because it was risky. Remember, for boys, behavior that isn't risky isn't worth doing.

How does this group differ from a gang? The difference is that gangs actually separate boys from their families, creating rules and rituals that tie the boy to the gang. Additionally, gangs usually have some form of threat to hold over the members so that they will not be tempted to leave the gang. Because these groups are held together by threats, they are very paranoid about the possibility that other such groups will attack them. The risky behavior now involves life-or-death actions that are justified by the need to defend the group. That is what you don't want your son involved in.

What your son's group needs is something to do that is risky, honestly risky. They are a bit young yet to volunteer to go to a third world country to build schools, so what they need is something that is active and requires their initiative. The projects that boys complete to earn their Eagle Scout ranking in Boy Scouts are exactly what many other boys need to do. If that doesn't appeal, seek out organizations that can use the energy and inventiveness of a boy this age. Social service organizations will benefit a great deal from the energy that boys have. Whatever the activity is, it needs to be real, the boys need to be an active part of planning and execution, and they need some freedom to do it on their own. If your son cannot find a constructive place to focus his energies, he may be interested in an activity that is seriously risky. The information in the appendix, "Weapons of Mass Destruction," will give you a hint of some things that will interest your son and his friends at this age.

PRIVACY

One of the effects of the personal fable is the middle schooler's desire for total privacy. You will hear your child say to his friends that he has no privacy and he is not allowed to do anything on his own. You know that is not true, but remember, it is all about perception. An additional problem is that some days he wants to be around you and the rest of the family and other days he retreats into his room.

If you say you don't understand which he wants—and that is totally reasonable—he will reply that you have no idea what he has to put up with. Just accept the child who wakes up any given morning and make no references to the child who went to bed in his room last night.

Speaking of his room, by the way, it's likely to be a total pigsty. He will lose things, he will blame people for taking his stuff, and he will be totally incredulous at your insistence that he tidy it up. Never succumb to the temptation to do it for him, although the threat of doing that can motivate him to clean up his room on his own. By the way, his backpack and his locker at school will look very much the same. I think that part of this is a need to put his stamp on his possessions, and if they are neat they don't look like his. Deep breath; it will get better, but not soon.

You can make your son dump his backpack out every Sunday night as a way to keep that moderately organized. It is astounding what he will find when he does that. However, let him do it; don't violate his privacy by doing it for him. You can require that there be no food or empty food containers in his backpack or room. The threat of bugs in the rest of the house is real, and he can at least have some consideration for the rest of the family and keep things food free. Point out that as long as he keeps his room so that there is no smell coming out of it from rotting food or overly dirty clothes, you will stay out of it. And, by the way, do him the courtesy of knocking on his door when you want to talk to him.

Use his need for privacy to get him to do his own laundry. He is certainly old enough now, although you will need to supervise him for a while. Point out that when he can do his laundry correctly he will have total charge of his clothes. Everything that you can do to encourage independence in your son means that he will be less inclined to shut you out. It is worth the effort it will take to teach him how to do his laundry. You don't want your son being like the college students I have known who mailed their dirty clothes home so that their mothers could clean and mail them back!

ELECTRONIC DISTRACTORS

Your son will spend a lot of time in his room, but do not let him have every single gizmo in there. At the very least, please do not put a TV in your child's room. When there are a limited number of TVs available in a house, children learn to negotiate and compromise when dealing with other family members. This is the perfect place to teach those skills. Everyone should be given a chance to determine what is seen, and older children should not be allowed to park in front of the screen simply because they are big enough to enforce what they want to watch.

It's entirely possible that members of a family will not spend time with each other if there's a TV in each bedroom of the house. Over and over, experts recommend that parents who let their child watch TV should watch the program(s) with the child. If something comes on that you don't approve of or needs to be explained, you are there for your son or daughter. If he has a TV in his room, you cannot enforce any prohibitions about shows you do not want him to see. Furthermore, when your son has homework, he may watch the TV in preference to doing his assigned work.

If your child whines or complains that "everyone else" has a TV in their room, your reply is simple: "I'm not everyone else's parent, I'm yours. And I don't think it is right for you to have a TV in your room." What you don't see is what happens in the classroom when a teacher makes some remark about the problem of children with TVs in their rooms. Then your child will brag about your rule.

For some of the same reasons, computers and other devices that connect to the Internet for all children under 18 need to be in family areas. Despite parental control software, clever children are able to get on to Internet sites that are not recommended for them. If your tweens complain that they want some privacy when they are on Facebook, point out that you are there to make sure others do not take advantage of them. They will scoff at this statement; after all, they know how to spot fakes. Direct your child to look up Facebook scams, Twitter scams, or whatever social network he likes at the moment. By the way, if you want to see a list of all such sites, just search for the social network site list on the Internet. You'll be astounded at how many there are.

If your son likes gaming, the needs of the rest of the family for access to the computer will cause friction. Having a computer that isn't connected to the Internet but can be used for computer games can help the family get along. In addition, small devices that are not exactly computers are now available on which a child can play electronic games and these can be very useful. Most families will give the device as a present and the child is responsible for the purchase of any games. I would suggest that you do it the other way around. That way the child is aware of the cost of the device and is more likely to take care of it.

When your child gets to the age when he needs computer access to the Internet to do homework or research for school, there is no reason why that has to be done in his room. When (if?) he goes to college, much of his research will be done on public computers in the library or other similar sites, and so he might as well get used to doing that now. Many teachers now require students to do work on the Internet, and if this is the case for your children, you may need to have some way of equalizing the amount of time they spend on the computer. Don't forget that computers are usually available in your public library, which anyone can use to do research.

The other reason for not having a computer in his room, even if it is not hooked up to the Internet, is computer games. At the very least, if your son plays computer games, you need to be aware of how much time he spends doing that. I promise you this: almost any game your son wants to play is not educational, and the skills he will acquire have only been shown to be of benefit if he becomes a jet fighter pilot, an air traffic controller, or a surgeon. I'm not suggesting you ban all computer games, but limit the amount of time your son spends playing the game. Encourage him to engage in games that require interaction with others in the same room.

With the melding of phones and computers, it is very likely your son has a phone that can play video games and can be used to view movies. A middle school child should probably not have such a device; give him (or better yet, have him save for) a phone with limited access to family and friends. A phone is a very accessible time waster, and the less it will do, the faster he will get bored with it. Some families require all members to drop their phones into a basket in the kitchen or the family room when they come in the house as a way to limit the amount of time children spend on the devices. In the old days, when all phones were corded, children had to talk to their friends in full view of everyone else in the house and that wasn't such a bad thing.

MELATONIN

Remember from chapter 2 that your brain does not produce enough melatonin to let you go to sleep for about half an hour after you watch anything with a bright light, and that includes TV and computer screens. So make sure that children turn off all screens at least 30 minutes before you want them to go to sleep. When middle schoolers have their computers and smartphones in their bedrooms, it's impossible to monitor that those devices are off. Many children who have problems in school have not had sufficient sleep. One other problem with melatonin is that when children begin puberty, their brains do not clear melatonin from their brains as quickly in the morning as they used to. So even if a child has had sufficient sleep, he may still be groggy in the morning. They sleep late and then are not ready to go to bed on time. Good sleep habits are essential for school success.

Adolescents identified with circadian rhythm problems are a growing issue in middle and high schools today. This isn't a common disorder, but the average day for some preteens and teenagers appears to be longer than normal. As a result, over time their sleep schedule migrates so that they are sleeping during school. There doesn't seem to be a good understanding as to the reason for this problem, but if your child is sleeping during school, is very hard to wake up, or is staying awake very late at night and this is a chronic problem (not just something on weekends), it might be good to ask his doctor about scheduling a sleep study.

LACK OF VERBAL ENGAGEMENT

Language development is key to success in school. If a child does not have a lot of practice in conversation, when he gets to school he is going to be at a disadvantage compared to other students. As with all skills, talking takes practice, and the child who is plugged into a video or a game lacks exposure to the opportunity to develop that skill. A great deal of the learning process requires good listening and good expression of thoughts. Remember, girls have an advantage in verbal skills, so your son needs time to develop his skills so he can keep up in class.

LACK OF PERSONAL ENGAGEMENT

Go into a room where a lot of children are watching TV and it is a bit frightening. All eyes are on the screen and there is no interaction among the children. When they get to school, these children have few interpersonal skills and do not know how to get along with others. They only know how to do things their way. Fighting with your siblings may drive your mother nuts, but you learn how to stand up for yourself and how to share toys.

Firmly restricting time watching TV, playing video games, instant messaging or texting friends on the Internet or an iPhone may sound as if you are in total control of your child's every move, as if you're imposing a "police state" in your home. Well, yes, of course you are! That is your job for a while, and even when you no longer are in control, your child will think that you are. Children need firm boundaries within which they are allowed total freedom. That makes them feel safe. In fact, the struggles you may remember with your parents over rules and regulations are what helped you attain your independence. Children who never have to challenge parental edicts may not ever leave home because everything is going their way and they have few responsibilities.

"But I don't want my child to leave home." Oh yes you do. Remember how much you disliked your parents' interference in your life? Your child hates it too. If we don't learn to struggle, we can't survive when times get tough. Those who can fight for themselves will do much better than those who are handed everything.

VIOLENCE AND COMPUTER GAMES

I had it easy. When my son was little, electronic games were not as accessible or as cheap as they are today. *World of Warcraft*, the most popular game with adolescents, is available online for a modest monthly fee, so all that is needed is a computer connected to the Internet and a parent's credit card. The burning question parents really want to know is whether or not computer games are bad for their children. The answer is both yes and no, and the evidence for this is not clear either way.

Computer games are bad

Violent video games are not appropriate for very young children. Period. Research has demonstrated that exposure to the most violent games does result in violent behavior. The question is, how long does that violent behavior last? No one really knows yet. An increasing number of studies indicate that there is a connection between playing violent video games and an increase in aggressive behavior. Furthermore, there is some evidence to indicate changes in the brain as a result of playing video games. However, there is no indication that playing an aggressive game like ice hockey doesn't also result in similar brain changes.

Computer games are good

As a result of playing video games, children definitely develop skills that they do not acquire in any other setting. Girls and boys who are familiar with such games are therefore familiar with computers and are usually facile with many different aspects and uses of both the hardware and the software. The more that education moves toward virtual education—online classes—the more the computer savvy child will shine.

What is the real issue?

The major problem with computer games is the amount of time children spend sitting in front of one, staring at a monitor, which results in a lack of interaction with other people. My students who identify themselves as "gamers" and most of those students are boys, have limited interpersonal skills and limited physical abilities. Yes, they may be sitting next to each other while they are playing a video game, but the only interaction between them is in the context of the game. Sitting for hours in front of the computer means that the only physical activity they get is in their arms and thumbs. It is obvious many gamers are out of shape and some are overweight as well.

The majority of experts believe that watching a lot of violent movies and playing a lot of violent video games makes children numb to the effect of the violence; consequently, the children see little wrong with the violence. As I mentioned above, there is an observable increase in violence in children who are engaged in virtual violence, but it may be due to lack of interpersonal skills and a self-absorbed view of the world, which may be seen as something the child can manipulate at will. What this means is that you probably want to preview a game before your middle schooler is allowed access. Don't take another parents' word for it, either. What may be acceptable to others may not be acceptable to you. (In the resources list, you will find the Internet addresses of sites that will help you decide whether to approve of a game or not.)

Another issue that has received attention recently is that some individuals become addicted to computer games or to just being on the computer. The evidence suggests that the pleasure center of the brain, which is involved in addictive drugs, is also being affected when these individuals play computer games. If you think your child is spending too much time on the computer, check with his teachers to find out what they think is the average time boys in your son's grade level are playing on the computer. If your son is on the computer more than that, pull the plug.

The solution is to allow your son a limited amount of time for video games. That time should not be at the expense of his schoolwork or as a result of his not doing anything else with his life. All children need at least one after school activity of THEIR choice (not yours) and for the "gamer" that may *not* be as part of a video gaming club. He may certainly do that, but he has to do something else as well. Anything you can do to encourage his involvement in an activity that does not include his gamer friends will be an advantage. Music, art, sports, and community service are all good choices. Many children who are gamers are also involved in skateboarding. The balance and coordination skills learned in riding a skateboard are great, but as I mentioned in an earlier chapter, just make sure your son understands basic safety rules.

VALUE OF MONEY

We all need to learn how to manage money and that includes earning it, saving it, and spending it. I introduced the subject of an allowance earlier. Make sure the amount of spending money you give your child is appropriate to his age and the financial state of the family. I can remember complaining as a girl that my allowance was smaller than my friend's allowance. My father pointed out that he was a teacher and made a lot less money than my friend's father did who owned his own business. My allowance was a portion of my father's salary, not my friend's father's salary. If I needed more money I would have to earn it. When I was in high school, I babysat and typed papers to make my spending money. Careful habits in handling money, learned young, will be valuable when your son grows up.

The two steps to learning the value of money that you began teaching your children early on definitely need repeating in discussions with your tween or teen.

1. Don't waste your money
    - Don't buy cheap items that break easily unless you can afford the loss.
    - Don't spend money to impress other people. If you do that, you will lose what you do have.
    - Keep track of your money and save some every week, even if it is just pennies. You might give your son a high-tech version of a piggy bank in which to keep his change.

2. If you don't have enough money, earn it.
    - Decide whether you need the item or just want it. If you just want it, save your money because soon something else will surely come along that you want too.
    - If you need the item, search around to see if you can find it at a lower price. Introduce your son to yard sales, junk shops, used sports equipment stores, and all of the Internet sources for buying older items.

If you are an impulsive buyer, your son will learn that behavior also. My father was addicted to junk shops and never left one without buying something. I've had to learn to stay away from them because I will do the same thing. My concern that I not waste money has rubbed off on my son, I'm glad to say, and he is a devotee of thrift stores and consignment shops and has furnished his house from those stores.

Help your child see the connection between earning money and spending money. As he gets old enough to have ideas about his clothing and his personal items such as shampoo and soap, give your son a clothing allowance to purchase some of these items. I always offered to buy the big-ticket items, such as shoes and coats as well as dress clothes, but our son had to buy the rest.

If you hand your child all the money he wants, you turn into the Bank of Mom or the ATM of Dad. As long as you are willing, your son will take the money. You can make unexpected gifts of money, but they should be modest. What you want is for your child to understand that money is something he should be working to earn. These days, gift cards are a great way for parents to give children money for specific purchases because it allows them the chance to learn to manage the money.

Why do you need to do this? For three very good reasons.

1. Children need to learn to respect what money can and cannot do. If they do not understand what money is all about, it becomes THE solution: just throw enough money on a problem and it will go away. Once children learn that the value of an item may not be in its monetary value, they will learn that money is not the solution to all problems.

2. Giving your child some money early will teach him how to keep track of money. One child I know got a dollar a week in allowance and asked for his father to give it to him in dimes. He could understand that three dimes would purchase a small piece of candy and that he got a bit of change back. When money is only in a credit card, it is too theoretical and has no meaning. Your son needs to be able to keep track of his money as well; teaching him to use a ledger or software on his computer to do so will reap benefits down the road.

3. Being in charge of some of your own money teaches you to delay gratification. Boys have more trouble doing this than girls do, and they need to learn early that if you spend all your money the day you get it, you don't have any until the next week. If you keep handing him money when he runs out, he won't learn how to manage what he has.

Suggestions From the Teacher

Children who can manage themselves by following through on class assignments and responsible for making sure that they get all information make better students no matter what their individual abilities are. You can help your child learn to be such a student by establishing early family routines and making sure that everyone follows through with their tasks and responsibilities.

CHORES

In middle school, a child is now able to take over essential household duties. Your son can make simple family meals, mow the lawn if your lawn requires strength to get the mower up and down hills, take the garbage out and put the can at the curb, and simple household repairs —starting with parental guidance, of course. You can depend on your son to be responsible for sorting the recyclables; the advantage here is that children who do so usually pay more attention to the problems of littering. This is usually part of the curriculum in middle schools and one area where what you learn in school has practical, immediate application in your life.

Remember that chores are something everyone in the family does, not just your son. Middle school children will complain that they are the only ones in their families who do anything like this, especially if there are older children at home. Because older children have more mobility, they are gone from home more and the middle schooler then tends to think he is the only one who does anything. If this is a complaint that you hear, move the chores around a bit so everyone has a chance to participate.

DISCIPLINE

As your child grows up, discipline changes. You used to have total control of your child and you don't any more. At this preteen/ tween/teen stage, what your child needs most is your presence. The parent who is around and paying attention to what is going on is more likely to be aware when something goes wrong. It is difficult to be aware enough of what your son is involved in to know what is going on with him and, at the same time, not be accused of prying. Establishing good lines of communication early is key here. If your son is used to sharing with you what he does and you are there for him that will continue.

What your son needs most from you at this point is structure and consequences. True, that has always been so, but particularly now. Consistency is also part of this. Be forewarned, you may think you are raising a future lawyer from the impassioned pleas for leniency and modification of house rules that you will hear from your son. It can be hard to stick to your guns when he gives you a carefully constructed list of reasons why he should be allowed to do something, which will probably conclude with, "All my friends are going." Give yourself a bit of time before you respond. Not with "We'll see," but with "I need a bit of time to consider this. I'll let you know tonight." That will give you the chance to actually find out whether all of his friends are indeed going. Probably not, but if they all tell their parents that story, it just might happen.

House rules should be short and general. Use the same sort of rules that schools use, along these lines: No hurting other people or yourself. Treat others with respect. Family comes first. And so on. If you actually produce a set of house rules, it can reduce the amount of arguments but it can also seem like a prison. The most important thing to remember about rules is that you can't change them. If you change rules then boys assume there really are no rules. Obviously, rules do change, but only for two reasons: (1) He is growing up and has earned a bit of freedom. (2) Family and school situations change and the present rules no longer make sense.

I said before that punishment should be linked to the offense and should take place as soon as possible after the child is disobedient. This can be more complicated as your son grows up because his life has more demands. If weeding the garden is the consequence for a particular violation and he misses soccer practice as a result, that is only fair if your son knew when he committed the mistake that he would miss practice. Assuming you made that declarative statement—"Do that one more time and you will stay home and weed the garden."—don't be conned into letting your son weed the garden at another time because missing soccer practice may get him in trouble with his coach. You are not being cruel, you are being consistent. If you made that statement about weeding being the consequence but you later agree that he can do it another time, the weeding is no longer a punishment. Your son has slipped out of the consequence.

On the other hand, if soccer is his life and he is very good at the game, it would have to be a very serious offense to warrant missing practice. What you see as very serious and what he sees as very serious are probably not the same. He will not see that failing to do his homework is that big of a deal, so point out that if he fails in school he won't be able to play soccer. There is nothing wrong with requiring an athlete to have decent grades in order to be allowed to play.

Your middle-school-age son is now involved in lots of activities that you are not a part of. Do not assume that because he is involved in a structured group with an adult leader that all is well. On the other hand, if you are not the supervisor, don't butt in. Your son will be very embarrassed. You need to be aware enough to be comfortable with what is going on but absent enough so that you are not asked to coach the team. This is one of the many places where being a parent seems like a balancing act.

Particularly in this context, there are four basic types of parenting (similar to those described by Baumrind (1966). If the parent is involved, she knows what the child is doing but is not necessarily part of the activity. (The counterpart, of course, is the parent who is not involved.) If the parent is responsive, he understands what the child wants and needs and takes that into account in making decisions. (The counterpart here is the parent who is not responsive.)

	Responsive	Not Responsive
Involved	Authoritative	Authoritarian
Not Involved	Permissive	Absent

As you'll note on the Involved-Responsive grid, there are four subcategories within the four basic types of parenting. Authoritative parents are firm about the rules but they stay involved in their children's lives. They know what is going on and insist that their children follow their rules. Authoritarian parents have no interest in their children's needs but they make sure that everything happens the way they want it to. Permissive parents let their children do whatever they want to do. For these parents, rules are more like suggestions, and their children rule the roost. Absent parents are just that; they are not available.

When we first discuss this topic in my psychology class, I ask my students whose children have the most trouble growing up, and they usually say those of the Authoritarian parent because they view that parent as being so mean. Once we discuss the material, they change their minds and say the children of the Permissive parent have more trouble because those children have no guidelines. In discussing this, my students come to realize that children of Permissive parents act up because they are looking for someone to care enough to enforce the rules. Children of Authoritarian parents may run away, but they were raised with rules and so can apply them in their own lives. Children of Absent parents simply go looking for other parents.

Yes, I know that it is impossible to be authoritative all the time. Parenting is probably the hardest job any of us do because it changes all of the time. Be aware of your children, be there for them, and be consistent and you will provide what your children need.

HOMEWORK

When your son was in elementary school, you were very aware of what he was required to do. He came home from school, probably showed you the work he was asked to do at home, and you supervised. Now that he is in middle school, however, you may be unaware of homework or projects except when you are asked to provide the materials for said projects.

As with everything else in middle school, this has its good and bad points. Your son needs to begin to become independent. After all, you don't want to be one of those parents who call up their son's college professor and ask for a copy of the syllabus so they can help. Don't laugh; those people exist. On the flip side, you know that your son is probably not quite ready to be totally responsible for his schoolwork and needs a bit of support from you.

That is the key point: support, not assistance. When he starts middle school, you will probably still be at the stage of asking your son what he has to do each night, but by the end of middle school, you should just tell him where you'll be in the evening if he needs help and leave him to do his work. If your child will not do his work unless you are sitting right by him, you are too involved. He needs to fail, and middle school is the perfect place for this to happen.

"You can't mean that!" I hear you wail. Absolutely. Boys generally are not well motivated by threats. So telling them that they will fail if they don't do their work does not help. What may have to happen is that they actually fail before they fully understand how much work is required to succeed. Children are self-aware enough at this age to figure out through trial and error how they work best. (Relax: no job application will ask for a middle school transcript.) If your son does his work because you are there hanging over his shoulder, he actually hasn't learned to do the work for himself.

What he needs from you is support, but not a lot of interference.

You need to provide a place where he can study. It should be reasonably quiet and free from distractions such as the TV. No, *he can't study better with the TV on*, but he might study better if he plays music. Music can help some children focus by providing a constant sound that covers up other distracting noises. The music works best if it is not too loud and it is somewhat hard to understand the words. Jazz works very well, and many boys really like that genre.

He also needs a regular time to study, and the whole family needs to respect that study time. This can mean that other family members don't watch TV or play loud music during that time.

When he comes home from school, your son probably would benefit from some activity. School requires a lot of inactivity and recall that boys *need to move*. What he needs for a while is something that is not sitting and doesn't require academic skills. That can be running errands for the family, looking after siblings, or some physical activity. What he doesn't need is to sit in front of the computer or TV.

If your son is having trouble in school, he needs you to listen. He may not actually understand what problem he is having, and it will help if he has to explain it to you. Just as they did in elementary school, boys will commonly complain that they hate school or their teacher hates them. This is their emotional response to the frustration they feel in not being able to do what they perceive everyone else is having no trouble with. You know your son's teacher does not hate him, but what he perceives is that his teacher is asking him to do things that don't make sense to him. Most teachers require students to study in ways that make sense to the teacher. They think the best way to learn is the way that they learn. This is the very reason why many boys have problems in school: they don't learn in the same way their teacher does.

VERBAL/AUDITORY VS. ICONIC/KINESTHETIC

Most teachers are verbal and auditory learners. As a result, they learn well from reading, from listening, and from writing. Most good students—and teachers were probably good students—have no trouble sitting still and following directions. If that doesn't sound much like your son, you have just figured out what his problem is in school. In elementary school, your son's teacher provided enough tasks that involved hands-on activities or lots of pictures to go with the words because educators realize the verbal skills of many young students are not strong enough to permit them to learn totally and solely from the written or spoken word. By the time children are in middle school, however, most teachers are relying on verbal messages to get the lesson across.

For a multitude of reasons, many boys are not good verbal learners. You remember reading in earlier chapters that their verbal skills develop somewhat later than in most girls and boys do not listen well either. Most boys are *iconic* and *kinesthetic* learners. That is, they learn best from visual representations and from physical involvement with the lesson. Those images, or icons, can be traditional pictures as well as numbers, charts, tables, and graphs. Boys can remember words better when they are graphically presented than when they are written out as in a book. An icon can be a chart that, although made of words, arranges the words in a pattern.

Kinesthetic learning involves hands-on activities, which is why your son may find math and science easier to learn. Such activities give him something specific to do. When he is asked to learn by reading material, he may have trouble with such passive acquisition of information. Simply listing what he is learning can help. That is partially why his teacher may ask him to write out the answers to questions or make a chart—both of which are kinesthetic activities. Handwriting may be an issue that interferes with his completion of such a task. Nevertheless, he should persevere. It is vital that your son do the work rather than sit by as you do it for him even though that may be neater and faster.

You can help your son translate his verbal and auditory tasks into iconic and kinesthetic ones. Here are some things you can do.

1. If your son cannot remember his assignments because the teacher tells them to him, make sure that he has an assignment book. Most schools require those even though many boys find it difficult to remember to write everything down. Many teachers will post assignments on a class website so students can access the information from home.

2. Have your son explain his lesson to you. Most teachers will tell you they remember the material they teach much better than the material they tried to learn. If he gets confused and can't seem to explain the lesson, have him go back a lesson and start there.

3. Work with your son to present the material he is learning into a chart or a table. For example, if he is learning about different forms of poetry such as haiku, limericks, ballads, free verse, couplets, and quatrains (this is part of the standards of learning for the state of Virginia for seventh grade), he can put the six different poem types at the top of columns and the rows of the chart can list how each poem differs according to number of lines, number of syllables, rhyme scheme, purpose, specific form, and the like.

4. Ask if someone at his school can show your son how to take notes by webbing. I'll bet his teacher has used that form in class, but he didn't realize what it was all about. This method shows the relationship among ideas rather than listing them in some sort of order, and the result looks more like a picture of words. If no one at school seems to know about this method of notetaking, you will find directions on the Internet under "note taking, webbing."

5. If your son has trouble paying attention to material from a textbook, have him read several paragraphs and then stop and tell you one fact he learned from that material. He should then write down that fact on a sheet of paper, or he can take his notes on a computer (which might interest him more). He should then read several more paragraphs and stop and tell you another fact he learned, writing that one down as well. The alternating reading input and talking output will keep his concentration focused longer than just passive reading, and the notes will provide a framework for review later.

6. Very active students find it difficult to just sit and read, so what they will do first is homework that is active, such as math, and then read. Have your son alternate his work, starting with a page of reading followed by several math problems. Moving back and forth will keep his activity level up. Some teachers are concerned that alternating a passive task such as reading and an active task such as answering questions means that the child does not focus sufficiently on either task. The writing is not the problem, however; the reading is, and many active children find that reading in bursts helps them focus better.

7. Sometimes it helps if a boy walks around while he reads. Remember that his system responds to stress with fight-or-flight and that means blood, sugar, and oxygen are sent to his muscles and his brain. Simply exercising his body means that his system steps up the delivery of energy to all parts of his body and his brain is getting more energy than it would if he was just sitting still.

8. The research on chewing gum is not clear, but there is some evidence that chewing gum helps memory or at least assists with maintaining alertness. Certainly being more alert will help learning, so it may help if your son chews gum while he studies.

9. Having something in their hand to squeeze has been shown to help boys learn better. You can get a gel-filled therapy ball or a foam object for your son to manipulate.

These are suggestions designed for home use. If your son finds that they help him study, he should be the one to ask his teacher if he or she will allow him to have his squeeze ball in class or to take notes in a web instead of the traditional format. What you want is to help your son become his own advocate. You help by providing suggestions and then, if they work, he implements them at school.

What do you want your middle schooler to be able to do?

- Be responsible for his stuff: his books, his clothes, his sports equipment, his toys.
- Spend some of his free time reading, some in a physical activity, and some with his family.
- Begin to do schoolwork on his own.
- Be responsible for chores and follow through with them.
- Start developing skills in an area outside of school.

CHAPTER 6

WHISKEY & CAR KEYS, TRUST & CONSEQUENCES: HIGH SCHOOL

The man who goes alone, can start today; but he who travels
with another must wait until that other is ready, and it may be
a long time before they get off.
—Henry David Thoreau

Giving money and power to government is like giving
whiskey and car keys to teenage boys.
—P.J. O'Rourke

So your son is in high school! There's a great deal of difference between a 9th grader and a 12th grader, but you may not see your son enough to appreciate that difference. While that isn't really true, it can seem that way. Your son will spend far more time at school, with his friends and with his activities, than he will with his family. What you will get is "Hi Mom and Dad, I'm off to school," and he will be out the door. It isn't that he doesn't want to talk to you, he just has a lot more going on in his life than he used to.

You need to be there for him, but not hovering over him, and managing that balance is hard. What will make this possible is if you and your son have developed good lines of communication up to this point. One way to maintain that level of communication is family routines such as eating dinner together at least four times a week. Remember, children who sit down to family dinners do better in school. If keeping to the schedule means you have to move the times around a bit and change one day for another, do so. It is important for your family to meet regularly. It won't be long before your son is able to get around on his own, so family schedules such as this will become even more important to keep you all connected.

At the beginning of high school, your son still needs chauffeur service. View this as an important time to chat with him, particularly because he may have moved into the front seat. So, don't use that time to catch up on your phone messages. Talk to your son about all sorts of things that interest you and you think will interest him. Topics can range from what you read in the newspaper, to his favorite sports team, to what he thinks about the ruling of the school board on school start times. You know that he doesn't quite yet have a firm handle on abstract thinking, but by talking with him, you model this sort of conversation. By talking with your son about ordinary topics, you are also telling him you are interested in him: you think he has valuable insights, and you are there for him. If you are talking on the phone as you drive you set a bad example for your son, both because distracted driving is not safe and this conveys to your son that your life is too busy to include him. Once your son is old enough to drive, you are not going to see very much of him, so use this time wisely.

If you live in the city and your son is getting around on public transportation, this time won't be available, so find things you and he can do together to allow you to have these conversations such as doing errands together or making your schedule fit his so you can ride the bus together. Also, if your son is doing anything you can watch him do, such as sports or an arts performance, be sure to attend. Going to and from that event together will give you time to chat.

Brain Changes

Our brains continue to develop and change our entire lives, but there comes a point where we consider individuals to have matured. On average, the male brain will not complete maturation until several years after the female brain, and you will see your son continue to change throughout high school.

VERBAL SKILLS

By the end of high school, your son's verbal skills should have caught up to that of the girls in his class. Some boys will be there at the beginning of high school and others take a bit longer. Even though boys can express their verbal abilities at the same level as girls do, this does not mean they process language in the same way as girls do. Research indicates that they don't. This may mean that your son does not understand what is said in the same way that a female understands a statement. The problem for some boys in high school is that they really don't get what their teachers say and they are too self-conscious to ask for clarification. The teacher may not understand the predicament either and tell you that your son is not paying attention to what is said in class, when rather he doesn't understand the way the information is being conveyed. Ask your son if he is having trouble understanding what the teacher is saying in class. He may well think that he has no skills in the given subject when the problem is actually a communication disconnect.

This may also mean that his male coach or his father may have a better chance at getting the point across to a teenage boy. Frustrating for the mother, but it's easier to accept if she understands it isn't that her son doesn't love her, he and she simply don't deal with words in the same way. Good teachers realize this and when a student doesn't understand something said in class, will ask another student to explain how she or he understands the information. Frequently just the different choice of words from another person is enough to clarify the situation.

There are other ways to deal with this situation. For example, the first step in creating a lab report for my ninth grade students in the boys' school where I taught was to make a list of the steps they did and then list what they observed. The relief of many boys in my class was almost comical. I've been asked many times, "You just want a list, right? No sentences?" I assure them that all that is required is a list, in the order of what they did, if possible. Once they can create accurate lists, I will show them how to turn a list into a lab report, but I know that many of them are so afraid of writing that starting with even a brief description of what they do is hard. Lists, on the other hand, because they do not involve complete sentences, seem easier even though the thinking process is similar.

If you have trouble getting your point across to your son or understanding what he is telling you, try this approach. Short sentences, which are basically lists of the information, may be more effective than long discussions. That can be a bit frustrating for adults who work better with a stream of consciousness approach, but clarity is worth the effort.

PREFRONTAL LOBES

The prefrontal lobe, right behind the eyebrows, is called the executive decision maker, and it allows us to make reasoned decisions and to control our impulses. Recent information suggests that this is the last part of the brain to fully mature, and the maturation rate is different between the sexes. The male brain develops more slowly in this area than does the female brain, and the best evidence suggests that females have usually developed their prefrontal lobes by age 18 to 22 and males by age 20 to 25—and maybe even 30! Boys have the reputation of being impulsive and risk takers, and this information on brain development explains in part why that observation is accurate. This isn't true for all males, but in general, adolescent males tend to act before they think.

Another problem resulting from the later prefrontal lobe maturity of boys is in how they make decisions. As girls mature through elementary to high school, their brains begin to shift from using the amygdala, which you will remember involves emotions, to managing emotional responses to using the prefrontal cortex. Boys, on the other hand, continue to use their amygdala until well into high school. The result is that girls are making reasoned decisions based on information and boys are making decisions based on their emotional connections. When faced with an emotional situation, girls will think it through before they make a decision, whereas boys are much more likely to act impulsively. It is thought that this may be the reason why girls are better able to delay gratification unlike boys, who are impulsive and not willing to wait for a treat.

The implications for this in school are huge. It is possible that girls' use of the prefrontal cortex explains why they will work for a teacher they do not like, but boys will not do so. It is very difficult to have a son who has done well in a subject all through school get to a high school teacher he does not like—or more likely he believes does not like him—and watch your son's grades plummet. A girl will study knowing that the payoff may be several weeks away, but if a boy doesn't see better grades as a result of his efforts within a week, he may decide the effort wasn't worth it. You probably can't change the way your son makes decisions, but you can teach him what the consequences are for bad decisions.

Most importantly, you must not rescue him. Yes, I know it is tempting to take his sports gear to school when he forgets it, but that takes time you probably need to spend elsewhere. Without his gear, he will get into trouble with his coach and teammates, and that might encourage him to remember his gear the next day. It isn't your problem when he forgets to tell you before Tuesday evening that he needs cupcakes for some event at school on Wednesday. If he doesn't give you enough time then he has to apologize for his error.

> **If you rescue your son, he will let you
> do that the rest of his life.**

Please don't forget that.

While some boys learn to control impulses by listening and watching others, many boys have to learn this lesson firsthand. If you are hovering nearby he will assume that you will solve his problems, so please give your son some space in which to make his own decisions and to fail. While the cost of failure is greater now that he is in high school, it is still less than it will be later in his life, and some boys seem to need to be at this level before they can learn the lesson.

Teens & Alcohol

Alcohol affects the prefrontal lobes and the cerebellum, which is why those under the influence cannot make reasoned decisions or control impulses or why they have balance problems. The by-products of alcohol digestion particularly affect undeveloped brain cells, which is one reason why binge drinking is so damaging to the brain. What is worse is that the part of the brain most affected by the effects of alcohol is the prefrontal lobes and, in particular, undeveloped tissue in those lobes. You now can see why alcohol is so devastating to the young male brain.

- The prefrontal lobes are responsible for making reasoned decisions and controlling impulses.
- Adolescent males are more likely to have undeveloped cells in their prefrontal lobes.
- Adolescent males are more impulsive and make fewer reasoned decisions because of the later development in the prefrontal area.

- Individuals who are impulsive and don't make reasoned decisions are more likely to binge drink.
- Alcohol affects brain tissue, especially the prefrontal lobes, by interfering with the process of cell development in the brain.
- The binge drinker selectively damages the portion of the brain that is involved with maturity.

Consequently, young males, who are most likely to be impulsive and take risks, are most likely to binge drink, which will injure brain cells, so their prefrontal lobes can't develop properly, so they will continue to drink, so . . . You see the vicious cycle. This may not happen with small amounts of alcohol because the toxins can be more easily excreted from the body and do not rise to levels that affect the brain. The major damage is done by binge drinking in the late adolescent or young adult male.

For the most part, every person's brain has completely developed by the late 20s, so your son still has some brain changes ahead of him. The ways he thinks and relates to the world are going to transform for some time to come. However, if you compare him to the boy he was when he entered school, he has come a long way. Just remember, he has a bit more to go, so while he can manage on his own at this stage, he still needs support from home.

PROCRASTINATION

Part of the failure to use the prefrontal lobes to make decisions is the tendency to wait to do something until the deadline is imminent. Procrastination is typical of young boys, and it drives their parents and teachers mental. One consideration is that boys wait to act because doing things at the last minute is exciting. Doing tasks as they are assigned is boring, and boys are more likely to do anything if risk is involved. If that is the situation with your young man, set him intermediate deadlines and challenge him to meet them. If you have said that he has to have his room cleaned up by the end of the weekend, bet him a pizza of his choice that he can't get his laundry done, folded, and put away by the end of Saturday. Just getting the clothes managed will make his room easier to deal with, and he may actually be able to finish the job by Sunday night. Teaching him to break the mountainous task into molehills and chip away at those will go a long way to showing him how to cope with tasks that seem insurmountable.

Another aspect of procrastination is that males may self-handicap. This is the idea that you set yourself up to fail because, for example, if you don't study, how can you succeed? If you put tasks off then how can you possibly complete them? The young man has some fear that the task is impossible, and if he attempts it he is bound to fail. Self-handicapping means that you are certain to fail, but the failure is under your control. The solution is exactly the same as before: show your son how to break the task into bits that are doable. By the time he has done each part, he will find that he has finished the task. This is the idea behind putting paper clips on small portions of a book, a technique we talked about earlier. Reading the whole book seems impossible, but reading three pages is something he can do.

WORRYING

You may have observed that men and women worry differently. Women are said to ruminate, to think over and over about an issue. If a woman has this sort of thinking, she may have a hard time letting a problem go until the matter is resolved. Many men do not worry this way; they are able to compartmentalize their worries. They think about the problem for a while, but when some other matter comes up or they need to do something else, they are able to put the problem in a box, put it on a shelf, and devote their full attention to the new task. A young boy is likely to forget about any given problem and will need to be reminded about it. It isn't that he doesn't care about the issue; he just totally forgot because the worry was tucked away. He simply needs a gentle reminder that perhaps now would be a good time to revisit the problem.

One theory is that this is due to sex-specific brain construction, but there is a great deal of difference of opinion on this issue. Some experts believe that the female brain has more connections between the two halves of the brain, which allows women to think over and over the same topic, while men are better able to shift gears, so to speak, and move on to another topic. Other experts are just as sure that this difference is learned and that both men and women can learn to worry effectively. Whichever is correct, your son may need to be reminded to reconsider some of the problems in his life; it isn't that he doesn't care about finding answers to them.

One technique to institute is a problem chart. This is a piece of paper that is divided into at least four columns. The headings for the columns are: Problem, Deadline, Roadblocks, and Solutions. When your son has a problem to solve, such as how he is going to complete his project or how he can earn enough money for the latest technology he is determined to get, have him write the problem down on a sticky note and put it on the chart in the Problem column. Then he should write the deadline for solving that problem on another sticky note and place it in the Deadline column. By the way, this is not the deadline for the problem but the deadline for solving the problem so that he can do the work.

The next step is to write at least one roadblock to solving the problem and one solution on sticky notes and place them in the next two columns. Each day until the deadline he should look at the chart and add to the last two columns. You need to tell him that problem solving is a process that takes time; letting ideas incubate helps. We are not always aware that we are thinking about problems, but over time the solution can come to us in an "aha" moment. In order to make sure that process occurs, we need to remember to think about problems regularly.

Why do I recommend using sticky notes instead of writing this directly on the chart? Two reasons. One is that it is hard to write on a chart that is stuck to a wall; writing on the note is easier. Second is that much of this process changes over time. Deadlines get moved up and back and roadblocks change as solutions are discovered. What you want him to understand is that worrying is a positive process. Making the process something that he can *do*, not just think about, makes it hands-on and concrete for him.

The Senses

The differences in senses still exist at this age even though the intensity of the differences may well have been learned over time or at least affected by the passage of time. For example, evidence points out that at birth boys' ears are slightly less sensitive to sound than girls' ears are. Over time, boys may have gotten used to louder sounds even though by high school their actual sound sensitivity may have equalized.

HEARING

A boy's need for louder sounds becomes a real problem when he discovers the latest music for his generation. Boys bother their parents and even the next-door neighbors with the levels of sound they feel are important to fully experience their favorite group. Years ago, my husband and I were houseparents in a boys' boarding school. The school's garage band practiced in our basement, and we were constantly reminded of their need for volume. When one member of the band got a new electric bass and cranked it up to see what it would do, we were amused to discover that the toilet paper in the bathroom above them had unrolled due to the vibrations.

The problem with very loud noises is that permanent damage may be done to the very structure in the ear that is transmitting sound waves to the brain. Eventually, that will result in noticeable hearing loss or deafness. Pete Townshend of the Who has serious hearing loss that he attributes to years of using headphones and standing in front of large sound amplifiers. Phil Collins has retired from touring because of the damage to his ears from the loud noises on stage. Many other rock musicians have sustained permanent hearing loss as well as ringing in the ears (tinnitus).

Are iPods going to cause deafness? The problem is not the device that produces the sound but the earbuds that deliver the sound to the ear. Earbuds are designed to be unobtrusive, and because they are designed to be as tiny as possible they are not effective in blocking out sounds from the environment. In order to hear the music clearly, the listener then increases the volume to overcome the ambient noise. If those around the listener can hear sound from the earbuds, the volume is probably too loud. However, if the sound is reduced, the listener is likely to complain that he can't hear the music because of the other sounds around him. The solution is noise-cancelling earphones, which totally surround the ear. Then the listener does not have to have the sound so loud. Even though they are large, unwieldy, and expensive, there is some indication that adolescents may be switching to those types of earphones. The difference in sound quality is enough that it is worth the bother of using the noise-cancelling type. In any case, experts suggest that earbuds be used for no longer than an hour at a time and at a level which is not noticeable to those around the listener.

This is a serious matter. The type of deafness that will result from constant exposure to loud noises is permanent, and it means that individuals using these small devices will get progressively deafer as they age. Worse yet, hearing aids will not overcome this type of deafness. Recent research indicates that many more people are suffering permanent hearing loss than used to be the case, and the belief is that this loss is primarily due to amplified sounds. Earbuds are not all that comfortable, so if you can get your son to use larger earphones, you will be doing him a huge favor in the future. At least give him a set of the larger headphones (noise-cancelling if you want to be generous), and ask him to use them when he is in his room. (Now, if I could just get that point across to the fellows with massive subwoofers in their cars.)

Recently, I discovered a pair of noise-canceling earbuds that are available on the Internet. They work moderately well and do allow the listener better sound quality than the standard earbuds do. They are not inexpensive, of course, but they do cost much less than the variety that cover the ear entirely.

What surprises many people is that boys seem to need to have noise or music on all the time and that noises don't seem to bother or distract them. As I shared with you earlier, some evidence indicates that girls listen to voices, music, and noise and boys listen to voices and music. If this is so, then boys really don't hear the noise which is why they are surprised when you ask them to stop tapping their pencil or squeaking their chair. They need to be a bit more aware of the fact that they make noises, but don't get irritated because they seem to be oblivious of such distractions and that is normal.

You may also have noticed that your son does not seem to listen to you; at least he has a hard time remembering what you know you told him plainly. Boys can be overwhelmed by too many words, so remember to keep the message short if you want your son to remember the directions as to what he is to do for you tomorrow. Make sure that you speak loudly enough, but do not yell. Yelling means that he won't pay attention because he perceives the negative tone. This is the place for a family bulletin board or a family calendar that can be shared on everyone's phone. If you don't know how to do this, ask your son to show you how to send messages on family events.

Other Developmental Hurdles

As your son develops, he manages his life better and needs you less. However, there are areas where as his parents you can be of great help because you have been there before him. Just don't make it too obvious.

SUPPORT VS. INVOLVEMENT

One of the trends that teachers have the most trouble with in high school is the growing number of parents who hover. They are referred to as *helicopter parents* and the statement has been made that their children can't wipe their noses without their parents reminding them to do it and handing them a tissue. This has gotten to be a huge problem in school because the parents are way too involved in their children's lives. By high school, children need to be pretty much on their own, making their own decisions and guiding their lives. If parents are doing this for their children—the parents of boys are more likely to hover—the boys will end up living in their parents' basement at age 30, playing video games.

"But," I hear you say, "my son won't do anything for himself." If that is true, it is probably because you have been doing it for him all along. As I've been telling you, boys are pragmatists; they are not going to do anything that someone else will do for them. They are not lazy; they are just not going to spend energy when someone else has offered. If you are a helicopter parent it is going to take conscious effort to break the habit.

Why do parents hover? One theory is that when boys were very little, parents were so concerned their impulsive boy would hurt himself they followed the boy around doing things for him that might have any risk involved. These parents seem to believe that children of good parents don't get hurt. What the boy needed, however, was looser supervision and the chance to learn from his mistakes. If you try to pick up something that is too heavy and it drops on your foot, you are likely to get hurt, but you are also going to be more careful in the future in picking up heavy objects. If your parent grabs it out of your hand, you never learn the effect of falling heavy objects until much later, when the object may be lethal. You likewise get the impression your parent believes that you are not competent to manage heavy objects. In their attempt to save their child from getting physically hurt, parents actually hurt their child's self-confidence.

Another theory of why parents hover is that they were the products of broken marriages and suffered because their own parents were so involved with their marital problems they had little time for their children. These children then linked with their friends and raised each other. They are terrified that they will do the same thing to their children and so hover over them so their children won't be left alone as they were. The complicating part of this is that these parents were linked to their friends, and so they all check with each other constantly about parenting skills. If one parent hovers, they all hover.

How do you know if you qualify as a helicopter parent? It is not so much that you are involved in your child's life; it is the intent to do for your child that is the issue. Hovering parents do things for their child that the child should be doing for himself or that don't even need to be done. Most importantly, the child should be learning independence and life management skills; with a hovering parent, there is no opportunity to acquire those skills.

By the time a child is in high school, parents should no longer be managing their children's academic lives. The only part that parents should play in schoolwork is in providing a place for children to study and in paying for the more expensive materials needed for projects. You can be a sounding board for ideas, make suggestions about strategies and approaches, and help with memorization tasks. What you shouldn't do is sit down with your son every night to do his homework. If he is having trouble, he will be better served by a tutor than by you. That way, your son is responsible for getting his work together to be ready for the tutor. Emotional connections make academic help sessions a difficult process between parent and child. Besides, your child needs to learn to solve his own problems, and if you help, he is not doing that.

Most helicopter parents do not recognize that their interference in their son's life is injurious to his development. They keep doing everything they have been doing all along and their son is perfectly willing to let them do it. If you say to yourself that you are helping either because your son won't do it or because he does a bad job, you are probably hovering. I was headed toward being a hovering parent and our son dealt with that by going off at age 12 to attend a choir school. While I don't recommend leaving home as a solution for hovering parents, I was totally amazed at all that he could do for himself. At age 12, our son could pack his own suitcase, keep track of his books and homework, do his laundry, fix a meal for himself, and write a check and keep a checking account. Because the school was at some distance, he lived at school and took a four-hour train ride by himself to and from school for vacations.

Your son can do all of that as well. By seeing to it that your son is responsible for himself, you will find that his relationship with you is not adversarial. In retrospect, I was constantly reminding my son what he had to do and then standing over him to make sure that he did it. Boys need to be independent and they need their parents to prepare them for independence. If you don't do that, he will pull away from you to join those you may not be thrilled with but who are treating him as an adolescent not a child. If you give him a well-prepared push out of the family nest, he will come back. Promise.

Suggestions From the Teacher

While there is less you can do for your son now than there was earlier, your son nevertheless needs you very much in certain areas. The trick with all of these is to be alert to his situation and offer help, but to back off when he no longer needs you or refuses your help.

CHORES

A high school student can do anything an adult can do, and a family rotation chart that involves everyone will make doing chores equitable. In fact, you should be able to depend on your son to help with a lot of the chores around the house.

If you have younger children, your son can be responsible for chauffeuring his siblings around, but only if those duties do not interfere with his own schedule and only if he understands the seriousness of taking care of that cargo. Being given the responsibility of taking care of siblings can help him start to develop a sense of personal responsibility. Driving young siblings is a chore that requires great care and most of my students will agree that they drive differently with friends in the car than they do when taking their little brother to soccer practice. At the very least, your son should be cognizant that if he agrees to drive his siblings, he needs to exercise great care and follow such rules of the road as making sure that all children ride in the back and are buckled up. I have known many families who count on their teenagers to provide this service. Be careful not to turn your son into an unpaid babysitter or tutor for his siblings, however. Yes, he can help drive them around, but everyone in the family with a driver's license should share that responsibility if capable.

The assumption in families is that when girls reach this age they should be expected to take over household chores, but boys are somehow exempt. The girls in my high school AP Psychology class frequently describe the duties they perform, from cooking the family meals to babysitting nieces and nephews. Rarely do I learn that one of the boys has similar duties. In the few cases where that is true, the sense of responsibility and worth the teens gain from these chores is obvious.

You will find a description of some of the issues of driving at the end of the appendix, "Weapons of Mass Destruction." However, using your high school student to run errands is a good way for him to learn to use an automobile responsibly. He should not be driving around with a lot of friends in his car. States that have rules limiting the number of unrelated people a teenage driver can transport point to the lower number of accidents by teens resulting from that rule. If you need your son to go to the grocery store for you, he gets the chance to drive, you give him responsibility, and he may be less tempted to drive his friends around.

DISCIPLINE

Early in high school, the boy you are used to having around the house may change into someone you don't want to recognize. He doesn't seem to be able to make up his mind about anything and then gets furious with you when you point that out. It is as if he is desperately looking for someone to blame his troubles on and you may be identified as either not wanting to help or wanting to help too much. One theory is that this is the child letting go of the egocentric thinking in which he was convinced the world revolved around him. He is beginning to realize that he is not the center of the universe and that can be frightening if he has no idea what his place is in the world.

Pick your battles. Hair is not worth an argument. Let him do what he likes with it within the guidelines of his school: shave it, color it, braid it, or even make dreads (as long as those are kept clean). Hair grows out and nothing he can do to it is permanent. You may think it's awful, but the world totally understands that young adolescents go through these stages and it is not a reflection on you. Yes, I understand that you know that first impressions are important, but he does not think that is true and you are not going to be able to convince him otherwise.

If the subject of piercings or tattoos comes up, try my husband's wonderful solution. His point was that as long as we paid for everything our son wore, ate, slept in, listened to, and so forth, we had the right to say what he could do to his body. Once he was able to pay all his bills and he was independent from us, his body was his to do with as he liked. It delayed the onset of those more permanent adornments such that what our son now has is fairly modest. While he was in the throes of wanting much more obvious decorations, he could blame us for being unreasonable, but since we said that he could do it anytime he could pay his own bills, we weren't totally forbidding the practice. And, at some level, that was encouragement for him to start paying his own bills.

Don't buy your son clothes you know he won't wear; you will waste your money. On the other hand, you don't have to indulge him with clothes that offend you or that you think are too expensive. Provide him with the basics of jeans or other unadorned trousers and plain basic shirts. If he cuts them up or paints them, don't get upset. Anything else he wants to wear he has to buy out of his own money. You can require that he have at least one outfit that is appropriate for church, visiting his grandmother, or any other place where he is not the center of attention. Ask at that time, too, that he tone his hair down so it is not so obvious.

The need for some adolescents to have nonstandard hair and clothes comes partially from a need to separate from the family. If your son dresses as you do then he is just a clone of you. He needs to find out who he is. He has not yet realized that costumes are just that and they really don't change the inner man, so to speak. You also need to realize that just because he dresses like a vampire, he *doesn't actually think he is vampire*. He just wants to get a reaction from others. The other part of this is that by dressing like others in his group, he finds a place he has chosen to be. He can't choose his family, but he can choose his friends. Invite the vampires in to watch movies at your house, provide snacks, and get to know the boys and girls in this group. You may be the only parent who does so and they will love you for it. At the very least, you will know where your child is.

Simply being there is the most important part of discipline at this age. Your son values your opinion more than he will tell you, and if you are around, you know what is going on. There isn't much you can do at this point to change his behavior, but if you have done your job up to this point, your good opinion will have leverage and you can use that to help him control his behavior. Tell him you are proud of him when he acts responsibility. My students tell me that statement means the world to them.

When your child gets older, take advice from my students—grounding doesn't work. You can't control your teenager well enough to actually separate him from his friends because he sees them in school or when he is practicing sports. You may be able, however, to keep him off of his email, Facebook, or Twitter account if you know how to check up on his use of those devices. Depending on the sophistication of your mobile phone and Internet service, you can block all incoming calls or messages from anyone other than you. Yes, that will take some doing, so think twice before you use this version of grounding as a consequence. If you do use grounding make it stick and I doubt you will have to do it again. However, it is moderately easy to get a cheap pay-as-you-go phone, so even if you take his phone away you may not be actually limiting his access to a phone.

Grounding tends to result in resentment because boys of this age report that they get more social support from their peers than from their parents or from girlfriends. Because of this support, separation should have an effect, but the problem is that he only focuses on what you are doing to him and not that his behavior is the reason for the grounding. Talk with him and outline options. Point out that his behavior has been unacceptable and be very specific about the behavior. List the options for punishment, such as no Internet, no phone, no car, no being around his friends, and the like. Then ask him what he thinks is an appropriate punishment for his offense. What does he think should happen? This way you link the punishment directly to the offensive behavior and, at the same time, start to put the control for his behavior into his hands.

Additionally, if you enlist him in designing his punishment you reduce the resentment, because you didn't do this to him, he did it to himself. Point out that since he agreed to the punishment, he is on his honor to do without whatever he settled on. Make sure that you both agree on a time frame, which is part of the punishment. When you get close to the end of the time, ask him to talk about what it has been like not having his favorite video game and was that worth what he did. Remember, his prefrontal lobes are still developing and he needs for you to walk him through the process of learning how to control his impulses. But also remember that a lot of his behavior is just that, impulsive. He is not purposefully bad, usually.

Discipline at this age depends entirely on patterns you have established in the past, so it's vitally important to establish good lines of communication with your son early. He has to know that you are in charge, you do expect him to behave, and you have control. If he gets to this age and knows that you don't have control, almost nothing you can do now will change that. Military schools have made their reputations on their ability to work wonders with adolescents because they start from scratch. You can do it yourself, but it will take a huge amount of effort and probably professional help.

RESPECT

Having worked with adolescents in the classroom as long as I have, the single most impressive trait that I see is a student who respects himself, his family, and others. This is the young man who understands that he has a place in the world and that what he does affects others. He also understands that not showing respect results in his not receiving respect in turn. No matter what your son looks like or is interested in, if he shows respect to others, he will find that the world has a place for him.

One of the major reasons why people don't get along is that they don't respect other people. Part of your job as a parent is to make sure that your child understands that his approach to life is not universal and may not function the same with others. There are two ways for children to learn respect. One is by being on the receiving end of respectful behavior. If a child is not respected it is difficult for him to learn why it is so important to be treated with respect. If your son is in an environment where adults or others are disrespectful, do what you can to ameliorate the rude behavior. At the very least, if you have evidence to the contrary, make sure that your son does not take the behavior to heart and think that he is not worthy of being treated well.

It is equally important for you to respect your son from the time he is little. It is very tempting to point out our child's mistakes and errors in judgment, but remember that he does not see the world the way you do. Telling him he is wrong might have caused him to back off when he was little, because he thought that his parents were always right. Now that he is an adolescent, he knows you make mistakes as well, and if you point his errors out, he may defend himself by attacking you. Treat your child as you would an adult, understanding that he does not think or feel like an adult quite yet. He will make mistakes, but if you show him that you value him, he will be more willing to listen to you.

The second way for children to learn respect is from working with others in need. The child learns how to deal with others from watching the adults in the group and learns what it feels like to give of oneself. Many children are not given the opportunity and therefore never learn how important it is for all of us to share our skills and abilities with others. Knowing that you can make a difference in your life by making a difference in someone else's life is how we learn to be good citizens of our world.

Community service

One of the best ways for all children to develop respect for others is through community service. Even if your son's school has a community service requirement, working with his parents is the best way to make this a part of his life. This is something the whole family can do together and will build connections and memories that will truly matter later on. The important thing is that these activities do not require any special skills and don't cost you anything. However, your child will learn that he is important to the world.

What follows is a short list of the sort of activities I am talking about.

- If you are into recycling, make that a family trait. Each child can be responsible for different categories of trash. If you live in rural areas, adopt a section of road to keep clean. If you live in more urban areas, work with other families to keep nearby parks or streams clean.
- If there is an elderly relative in the family, your children will probably be very willing to go to retirement homes or senior centers. If this is the selected service, make sure that your children go on a regular basis—preferably once a week, but certainly more often than just at holidays.

- If your child has particular skills such as crafts or athletics, he can volunteer at a local day care center or community center.

It is amazing what community service will do for children. One young man got involved with Habitat for Humanity through his local church group and now is considering a career in construction. Another boy was roped into helping his math teacher with a Lego Robot competition and now is majoring in engineering. If children are only exposed to what is available to them in school and at home, they may never find their true interests. Community service has the double benefit of giving children real work to do that benefits others at the same time they themselves are developing skills in getting along with others.

After High School

You have been working so hard to get your son through high school that it may have escaped your notice that the end is fast approaching. Your son has several choices to make, and they are his to make. You can provide some information and help him sort through his choices, of course, but you are not to make his decision for him. I've been there; I know how tempting it is. The first option is, of course, further education, but there are several versions of that, including work-study and taking a year or two off before continuing on to higher education. If education is not a realistic choice, there are lots of other options; going to work or entering the military lead these choices.

You are a good judge of your son's abilities and you know what decisions you would make if you were in his shoes, but he is not you. He may share some of your abilities—or better yet, has abilities you wish you had—but his world is not yours, and the choices he makes should suit him. That last sentence has become almost a mantra for me in trying to remember that my son and I are not the same. If I were him . . . but I'm not, and his decisions are not going to be the same as I would make.

Many boys have had it with sitting in seats, doing what they are told, and reading. They want something more active to do, something that involves risk and interaction with the world. Some of these boys may opt to postpone furthering their formal education. The idea that their son may not go directly to college, however, can panic some parents. They are concerned that if he doesn't go to college right after high school graduation, he will never go back. Don't forget, if your son doesn't continue on with his education, he has wasted no time and you have wasted no money. If he really wants college, he will get in when he is ready.

Let's take a look, then, at your son's options if he is not going to attend a traditional four-year residential college.

TERTIARY EDUCATION

There are lots of other options for college other than four-year schools.

Two-year colleges are an excellent way for a student to keep connected to school while at the same time holding down a job full- or part-time. These schools understand that many of their students are what is termed *nontraditional*. In other words, they are older, not full-time, not interested in a traditional liberal arts course of study, among other factors. Junior or community colleges are a great place for your boy to find out if he is interested in continuing to stay in school at a price that won't break the bank if he decides against continuing.

Technical colleges provide training in skills for jobs and usually with some method to obtain those jobs upon completion of the program. Be very careful in selecting one of these because many have been fly-by-night organizations or have not provided quality training. One way to decide if a particular program is good is to find someone in the career that your son is interested in and ask that person what he or she thinks of the training provided by this school.

Online college courses are also a possibility, but I don't recommend them for a boy right out of high school. That form of education takes self-discipline, and the boy who is not ready to attend a physical school is probably not ready for a virtual school. If he rejects a physical school for financial reasons, please be forewarned that reputable virtual schools are not a whole lot less expensive than the bricks-and-mortar variety. The main advantage of online classes is that they allow the student to arrange his studies around a work schedule. For a boy who can manage a full-time job as well as some further education, virtual classes are ideal. The main disadvantage for a boy, however—for whom a group is all important, remember—is that going to school from your computer does not link you to peers to hang out with.

THE MILITARY

Many boys have found that the military provides the structure, self-discipline, and training they lacked in high school. I quite understand parents' concern about the danger involved, but nevertheless, this can be an excellent experience for young men. For some this is an acceptable way to get away from home. They want and need to separate from their families and the military provides a family to be a part of. The fondness of many older men for their military experience testifies to how important that connection can be for boys.

If your son chooses this option, do what you can to be a part of his decision-making process without hovering. See if he will let you serve as a sounding board because you will be able to offer some perspectives he may not have thought of. One of my students signed up for the service without being totally clear about his obligations. He is glad he joined up and is getting training in technology that he will be able to use after his service commitment is completed, but he did not know that he would have to stay in as long as he does. Make sure that your son is given the opportunity for training in a skill or occupation as a part of his service. Suggest that he discuss this with others who have served, especially those who have had recent experience in combat zones. Don't collect the information for him, but help him figure out who he needs to talk to. Most importantly, don't tell him you think the military is a bad idea for him, even if you believe it wholeheartedly; he will almost certainly pick that option if you voice your objections to it.

That is true for all of his decisions, of course. If you let him know that you think a decision is the wrong one, he is very likely to stick to that because he wants to prove to you he is capable of making his own decisions. It is a much better plan to have him explain his thinking to you and simply to ask a few (please note that I said a few) questions about his choice. Once he has made up his mind, make sure that you support him even if you think he has made the wrong choice. It is very hard to face your family when your decision turns out to be a mistake if they are there saying "I told you so." By the way, this also works when he brings a girl home to introduce her to his family.

WORK

If your son wants to go to work, he should be treated as any adult who has a job. What this means, practically speaking, is that if he continues to live at home, he should be responsible for taking care of his clothes, all of the contents of his room, any vehicle that he drives (together with paying for insurance and upkeep), as well as for paying you a portion of his room and board. By living at home, your son can save money toward being able to afford to live on his own later, but you should not support him totally. After all, there should be some incentive for him to move out. You should also sit down together and decide on house rules. He is living under your roof; will you allow him to entertain someone overnight in his room? (See the movie *Failure to Launch* if you want some idea of the problems of an adult child living at home.)

GAP YEAR

It is customary in other countries for children to take a year or two after finishing high school before they go on to college. Sometimes this can be in the form of mandatory national service; sometimes this can be a year overseas in a university program designed for such students, a year working in a social service organization, or a number of other programs. You will find a list of such opportunities in the resources at the end of the book.

If your son decides not to go to college, do not despair. We all know of many successful men who do not have a college education and many others who have gone back to college after some years of trying other possibilities. What is important is that your son makes his decision based on what he wants, not on what you think he wants or what you want him to do. He is, after all, almost an adult and should know that his actions have consequences.

Whatever your son does with his life after high school, you will know that you helped him learn to make choices and supported whatever he decided to do with his life. What you want is for your son to know that you believe in him.

What do you want your high school student to be able to do?

- Be independent in that he can manage himself and his school requirements.
- Be an active and productive member of his community.
- Be responsible for himself and for anyone who depends
- on him.
- Learn the process of making life decisions.

CHAPTER 7

A MAGNIFICENT WORK IN PROGRESS

A boy becomes an adult three years before his parents think

he does and about two years after he thinks he does.

—General Lewis B. Hershey

Men want power to do something. Boys want power to be something.

— Eric Sevareid

We have spent some time discussing the typical behavior of boys and how that affects their progress in school. Please remember that the operative word here is *typical*. Stereotypes exist because there is some basis in fact. No, not everyone in a group follows the stereotypical pattern, which is why stereotypes have a bad reputation. But stereotypes exist because many people in a group do appear to have similar behavior, and even if any group member's behavior is not typical, others outside the group will assume that the individual will behave like the group. To put this more concretely, boys in general are seen as creating problems in school, and even if your boy does not fit that model, some may take it for granted that he does.

What School Can Do for Boys

If boys perceive that the adults around them expect boys to have educational issues, this can give those boys permission—in their own minds—not to succeed. Good teachers and parents are aware of this possibility, however, and can take pains to ensure that the boys in their care do not fall victim to such a belief. You cannot control the influence of others on your son, but be alert to any statements from him like: "There is no reason for me to try, I can't succeed," or "School is not a place for me." If he believes that he cannot succeed, he will be correct. Positive thoughts are no guarantee of success, but with your support, his chances will really improve! We have spent a good deal of time talking about how you, as a parent, can help your son succeed in school, but what can you expect school to do for your son? Aside from stuffing facts in his head, schools are places where we all learn a great deal.

SELF-CONCEPT

From the very first day in school, we get impressions about how well we do compared to others. That is true at home as well, but family is different. Being compared to people you are not related to gives you some understanding of how you fit in the larger world. That can be a bit of a shock to a child whose family has been very careful to support just about everything the child does. All of a sudden he finds out that he isn't allowed to grab anything he wants and that he has to take turns.

As children develop, one of the first steps they take in developing their understanding of themselves is the separation from their parents, especially their mother. This can be a big step for the parents as well. They soon discover their child has likes and dislikes that are not the same as theirs. Take a moment to think back on your son's development. You may remember the moment when you realized he had a unique set of character traits, that he was his own person. The next step is for the child to realize that concept for himself, and one place that happens is in school. A very little child will come home and tell his parents that some classmate was silly because she didn't like peanut butter and jelly sandwiches, a personal favorite of the boy. He can't imagine that someone else doesn't like what he likes. This is an example of the egocentric view of the young child, which we discussed earlier.

As your son begins to pay attention to all of the differences in the children he goes to school with, he will start to develop a sense of himself, that is, his self-concept or his self-image. He finds out what he likes and what he doesn't like; what he is good at and what he has trouble with; who can be trusted and who to be suspicious of; and a host of other lessons as well. He needs to come home and talk this out with you as the person he trusts the most. When he says his classmate is silly for not liking PB&J sandwiches, what he is actually asking you is whether or not this food choice is a fatal character flaw. What he wants to know is whether or not that difference can be accepted or not. You didn't think about that when you tell him, "Well, honey, some people don't like those sandwiches just like you don't like bologna." This tells your son not all people are the same and that gives him information he didn't have before.

Yes, your son learns facts and concepts in school, but he learns so much about himself as well. It will start with the classmate who doesn't like PB&J and then move on to other facets about himself, such as which subjects he is good at. That will link into finding out how he approaches problem solving, which lays the groundwork for what he will do with his life. Astounding how talking about sandwich preferences starts the exploration of one's self, but it happens because he trusts you to accept him and help him deal with the larger world.

COMMUNICATION SKILLS: BIRTH TO THE BEGINNING OF SCHOOL

Because your child is a boy, his first focus will very likely be on developing physical skills. He will grab for something long before he learns to ask for it. He wants to touch and handle everything that comes in his way, and it may be hard to distract him. Every mother of a boy carries a stash of small toys to give her son in place of the candy wrappers he will pick up from the sidewalk. This doesn't mean that he will give up the wrapper immediately, however, and you may be amazed how strong he is when you try to take it away from him. Make the toy sufficiently enticing and he will drop the wrapper on his own. For example, while you wiggle the toy, say something like "See this, what do you think of this?" Hold the toy to catch his attention, giving it to him when he drops the wrapper.

Your job is to help your child acquire language, remembering that the language part of his brain is going to develop a little later than that of a girl of the same age. He will get there, but he needs a lot of language input from you. If he develops strong language skills in communication, that will make his transition to school much easier. In school, people are talking all the time, so the more your son learns to listen and to speak, the better prepared he will be for school. Some boys acquire language skills easily and early. If your son is one of these, he may have an easier time in school in that regard, but it's no guarantee of his success in school.

Your boy also needs to learn to control his physical impulses. Should he go to school thinking he has the right to grab anything that appeals to him, he may find himself in trouble with both the teacher and his classmates. By the time your child goes to kindergarten, he should be ready to leave an object alone or put an object back if directed to do so. He probably won't want to do that, but he should be able to follow your directions. The more you talk with your son, the more likely he will be to do this. The operative word in that statement is "with." Don't talk "at" your son; include him in your conversations even before he has acquired a lot of verbal skills. One of the best ways for boys to learn to communicate is by practicing with their parents.

Ask him questions about what he is doing, such as "What is happening with your cars?" Get him to express to you what is going on in his life. When he falls, for instance, don't ask him if he tripped. That gets a yes or no answer. Ask him what he fell over. Our son would trip over his own feet, so we suggested that perhaps he fell over a pile of air, and then we asked him if he could find that pile. He was intrigued and would stop crying as he looked for the mythical air. My husband would also ask him when he fell if his knee was "surprised" by hitting the floor. Even as a toddler, our son was amused by the notion of his knee shouting out, "Hey, don't fall on me!" Focusing on his knee instead of his reaction to his fall would totally distract him. Using language to help him manage himself physically taught him how to express himself.

Because many boys do not come to verbal skills easily, it is easy to allow them to continue to express themselves nonverbally or not at all. A friend recently noted that his teenage son has become a chatterbox now that his older sister has gone off to college. My friend was unaware that the sister was acting as a "translator" for her younger brother, reporting to her parents what the boy wanted. Now that my friend's daughter is gone, he is fascinated to discover that his son really does like certain foods that the boy's sister stated he did not.

What boys at this age need is to acquire communication skills, both listening and speaking, and physical control, especially of their hands and feet. Establish an emotional connection with your son and you will find that you have laid the groundwork for communication the rest of his life.

SEPARATION FROM FAMILY: KINDERGARTEN AND EARLY GRADE SCHOOL

Going to school can be fun. After all, you get to do things that are new and do those things with lots of other children. Some children can become overwhelmed, and if your child is one of these, help him make the transition by enrolling him in a nursery school several mornings a week. It won't help him if you hover and try to solve all of his problems, though; he needs to learn to deal with the people in his life. He is not the only child who feels this way, and educators understand how to help children who are slow to warm up to fit in with the group. Your son needs you to trust him to be on his own. Recall my oft-repeated warning in earlier chapters: when you hover, you give him the impression that you believe he can't manage himself, and he won't try.

It is important for you to let your son know that school should be as important to him as work is to you. Talk to him about how you manage the tough days at your job. This will help him understand that life is not always easy for everyone and we all have to learn to cope with difficult days. He will learn early not to give up, to keep trying even when he doesn't succeed. Young children believe that their parents make no mistakes. Eventually, your son will realize that is not true, but it will be less of a shock if you share some of that knowledge with him earlier rather than later.

During kindergarten and first and second grade is the time to establish the lines of communication about what is going on in school. Ask your son to show you what he learns in class each day; the review will help him remember what he was taught and your interest will help him know you care. The operative word here is "show" not "tell." When you ask him to tell you what he learned, he will very likely not be able to verbalize the information or he will give you a very brief answer. On the other hand, if you ask him to show you what he did in school, you will get an amusing glimpse into his life in school.

Please know that what he says happened at school and what actually happened at school are not necessarily identical. Your son may be telling you something he overheard from another child and the story may have altered a bit as it was passed along. Also, what your son says the teacher said to him may not be the unvarnished truth. I'm not saying your child is telling an untruth; what happens for all of us is that our personal filters can change how something appears. For instance, a child who was raised in a home with just a few family members, all of whom speak moderately, may believe that a teacher is yelling when she speaks loudly enough to get 30 rambunctious children to pay attention. I have a loud speaking voice, and some people might believe I am being aggressive when I am just loud. On the other hand, don't discount what your son says. Find out for yourself if you are concerned.

"My teacher hates me." Countless boys have spoken those words over the years, and rarely is that the case. Over the years, I have tried to figure out what could possibly be behind such a statement. These are the top four reasons I have discovered, among others.

- The boy was caught doing something he shouldn't do, such as not paying attention. The easiest way to cope with that is to blame the teacher.
- The teacher told the students to do something one way and it doesn't make sense to the boy or he can't learn that way. He hasn't told the teacher these things, by the way; he just assumes he or she knows he can't do it that way and is making him do it in a way he can't on purpose.

- The teacher has a low tolerance for wiggly boys and only interacts with boys to tell them to stop moving and pay attention. (By the way, this teacher is very likely unaware that he or she feels this way.)
- The boy got interested in some subject not related to the topic of the lesson. When the boy asked questions about this subject, the teacher declined to answer them and tried to get the boy back on the topic.

The first step is not to make a big deal about this. Some of the complaints from all children about teachers and schools are simply a trial to see if you were listening or to see if they can manipulate you. These remarks are similar to what a child would say if you told him he couldn't go to his friend's house to play because he has sports practice. Within half an hour at the practice session, he has forgotten all about visiting his friend because he is involved in the physical activity of practice.

If your son continues to complain about his teacher, then you need to find out exactly what precipitated this statement. Having established good lines of communication with both your son and the teacher will help. Frequently, the teacher will view the boy who is physically active and whose attention shifts when the source of information is verbal as having an issue, and the boy will believe that the teacher does not like him. The teacher probably likes your son just fine and is frustrated that such a bright boy can't seem to control himself in class. Ask the teacher what she expects from your son and what you can do to help, but remember that your son is responsible for his own behavior.

One thing that helps many boys maintain focus is to have something like a sponge ball to manipulate while they work, but the teacher needs to know why your son has one. Otherwise, she may see that item as a toy and take it away from him. She may substitute something that it is not a toy but still serves the purpose of letting the boy shuffle an object in his hand. I like small foam stars for this purpose because they don't lend themselves to being tossed like a ball, they are stiff enough to provide some exercise, and they are big enough not to get lost. Very wiggly boys sometimes benefit from being allowed to stand by their desks, sit on a large exercise ball, or walk back and forth in the back of the classroom. The challenge is getting the teacher to agree to these suggestions because all of them will make your son the center of attention for a while until the other children get used to what he is doing.

If your son has trouble learning to control himself he runs the risk of becoming the focus of class disruption and developing into the "class clown." There always seems to be one boy in every class whose physical reactions are the source of amusement for the rest of the students. Some of these guys have gone on to become professional comedians, but most do not. If your son thrives on this sort of attention, get him involved in a community theater or a children's chorus.

Boys this age need to begin to develop independence and to start the process of functioning on their own. I know you see your son as your little boy, but he wants to do things by himself. When you let him do so, suffering the consequences for his mistakes, you help him lay the groundwork for the next stage.

Make sure, too, that your son has ample place and space to run, wrestle, and generally engage physically with his environment. That is one way boys learn how to deal with their world. Remember, that the boy who has the opportunity to roughhouse has better social skills than the boy who does not. Boys tend to be noisy, messy, dirty, and physically involved with everything they come in contact with. If they are allowed to do that as boys, they are more likely to grow out of that stage than if they are required to be calm, quiet, and tidy. Give your son real tools to use as soon as he can. Shovels are great in a sand pile, but what boys really want to do is bang on things and take them apart. Make that happen. Boys will grow into men if they are allowed to be boys. See the appendix, "Weapons of Mass Destruction," for some guidelines on this subject.

SELF-MANAGEMENT: FOURTH GRADE THROUGH MIDDLE SCHOOL

As your son progresses through school, you will be less and less involved, and that is how it should be. You will still know what he is studying and what his major projects are for school, but you will not necessarily be involved in the day-to-day work in his classes other than to cast an eye in his direction to make sure that he is doing his schoolwork.

This portion of your son's life is the most difficult for you both. He no longer wants or needs the high level of involvement that you provided earlier, but he may not thrive if you treat him as you will when he is in high school. This stage requires vigilance without stifling, humor without making fun of him, and love without smothering. You need to know what he is doing but not seem to be directing what he is doing. In this stage, one of the best things you can do for your son is to surround him with adults who understand him and have his best interests at heart such as coaches, tutors, group organizers, and religious leaders. Let them interface with him while you interface with them, but let him know you are still involved.

Particularly early in this stage he will not be surprised that you know most of what is happening to him. After all, when he was younger you knew all about what he was doing, so it seems normal. As he matures and approaches high school, however, he may become more and more irritated with your need to know what he is doing. He will call it meddling, and his reaction will be to become more secretive. Trust those around him to do their job and only occasionally meddle in his life. Although this is your prerogative, don't abuse the privilege.

The best thing you can do for your son at this stage is to give him responsibilities and let him suffer the consequences if he fails to fulfill them. I have said it before: Don't rescue your child. If you do, he learns nothing except that he doesn't have to worry about what he does because he trusts you to pick up the pieces. What he needs from you is help in how to put those pieces back together himself. He needs to know that you had to learn the same lesson and that you lived to tell the tale. My students have been fascinated to find out that I got into serious trouble in middle school and that I survived. When I tell the story, I don't focus on why I did it, or how upset my parents were. Instead, I emphasize the lessons I learned about myself and how I changed so that I wouldn't fall into the same pit again. By this stage, your son knows you are not perfect; what he needs to know is how you managed your mistakes.

That is the lesson of this stage in your son's life—how to manage himself. It is so very hard for parents of a boy at this age to back off a bit because they know their sons are nowhere near ready for total independence while those sons think they are. On the other hand, boys at this stage are far more capable of running their own lives than you believe they are, and that is why your son's teacher can be a great ally in this process. If his teacher thinks he is capable of doing something, trust that the teacher is correct.

Science projects are a great example of how to help without taking over. The topic of your son's project should be his own idea. I don't care if you know of a project that would be really interesting, if your son has an idea that he wants to do, let him do it. If he comes asking for ideas, that is a different matter altogether, but don't volunteer topics unless asked. Your job is to act as a sounding board, letting your son tell you his plans. You may need to help him figure out an appropriate schedule, but it's really the teacher's job to help all of the students figure out when their intermediate deadlines will be. You will probably have to supply some materials, but help your son figure out how to adapt what you have around the house rather than rushing out to buy something. He will learn more about the project by repurposing found objects than buying objects made for the purpose.

For example, you can find a wide variety of Styrofoam balls at the local craft store that can be used for a model of the solar system, but it will be better if your son collects all the balls he can find in your house and use those. If the Earth is a softball, how big does a ball have to be to count as Saturn or the Sun? He will find that the scale of those is way too large, so perhaps he needs to start with a small rubber ball as the Earth and a very small ball of aluminum foil as the Moon. Not as fancy as the painted Styrofoam balls, but he will learn more. The point of a science project is not how it looks but what the student learns preparing it. When you are working with your son on his project, you don't want the teacher to give you the grade. (I have been tempted to do just that on occasion.) Your son must assume ownership. Remember, the point is *what the child learns* not what it looks like; your child should put more energy into the project than you do.

Another area where parents tend to insert themselves is into homework. The purpose of homework is for a child to try to do something by himself without the active guidance of his teacher. It is not to produce a perfect product. If your son turns in homework without errors because you edited or actually did part of his work for him, his teacher does not know that your son didn't do that work by himself. When he gets to a test, he may be unable to complete it successfully because he actually hasn't practiced doing the work on his own. The teacher needs to know when the student can't do the work by himself, and the only indication to the teacher that your son has trouble with the material may be the quality of his homework. Your job when it comes to homework is threefold: (1) to provide an appropriate place and time in his schedule; (2) to supervise him to make sure that the work is being done; and (3) to provide some guidance to help him figure out his answers. Your job is not to sit down with your son and answer the questions for him or to write down the answers.

Boys this age need parents who support them in their journey to become independent individuals. It is very easy to take over when your son gets frustrated or finds his work hard, but all that that accomplishes is getting the homework done, not having him learn how to do the homework. By the time your son enters high school, he should be capable of doing his work on his own with support from you on rare occasions.

FIRST STEPS TO YOUNG ADULTHOOD: HIGH SCHOOL

You probably don't think of your ninth grader as a man, and he doesn't either, but he is thinking at some level of the man he wants to become. He is beginning to figure out what his interests and abilities are now and what he will do with himself in the future. He may ask you when you knew you wanted to be whatever you are and how soon you began the process of getting there. Remember, at the end of high school, your son is considered an adult and is legally able to make life-changing decisions. Make sure he is ready for that by giving him the chance to make decisions for himself. Do not expect him to have all the answers for a long time even though he thinks he does.

The avenues of communication that you developed early in your son's life will help you keep in contact with him as he negotiates high school. He needs your guidance and your perspectives on life, but be careful about starting sentences with "When you grow up . . ." or "When I was your age . . ." He is not ready to totally think like an adult or to be given adult responsibilities, but he doesn't want to be reminded of that. Try the same information the other way around: "When I was in high school, one of the things I did was . . ." How is that different from "When I was your age . . ."? He can't wrap his head around the concept that you were ever his age, but he does know that you were in high school, so sharing your experiences is acceptable. It is all about perspective.

The major challenge for boys in high school is their impulsiveness. When they take time and think through an issue,

THE PARENTS' GUIDE TO BOYS

most can make some unbelievably grown-up decisions, but then they will turn around and say or do something that lets you know they are not grown up yet. Remember, the probable reason for this lack of consistency is that the prefrontal lobes, where the executive decision maker is, develop later in boys than in girls. Your son may get very upset with you because you will not trust him to do something responsibly because you remember the bone-headed move he made last week. He remembers the praise he got for some other behavior and complains that you don't trust him. Part of growing up is learning how to deal with the results of one's decisions, and if you protect him too much, he will never learn. Begin by walking through the decision-making process with him so he will learn the process. Then let him go. If you don't trust him to make reasonable choices, he will never learn how to do that. Start that process sooner rather than later.

Another pitfall is that if you don't trust him to some extent he may, out of frustration, make a big mistake. For example, if you are concerned about him driving with his friends in the car because they are distracting, you may set a rule that he is not to drive with anyone else in the car except family members. If he gets teased by his friends, however, who tell him he should take control of his life, he may just take his buddies for a ride after school some day and an accident may result because he was showing off. If you choose a moderate course and let him drive with one friend in the car, distractions are reduced and he still may be able to control the car.

This compromise is no guarantee, you understand, that he will be totally responsible with a car, but boys need some space in which to make mistakes.

By the way, he really doesn't "need" a car. Schools provide transportation. If he wants a car, he should make the money for it, but not at the expense of his schoolwork. Cars tend to be the watershed for boys, and for some of them, the desire for a car is visceral. Other teenagers are just not that interested. One of the advantages if you help with the purchase of your son's car is that you get some input as to what car he purchases. You want something safe and cheap, and he wants something fast and sexy looking. These two are not mutually exclusive. Make it his job to find his car; don't do it for him. Be part of the decision-making process—after all, you are providing some of the purchase price— but in the long run, he is the one who will hold the title. Part of his research should also be to find out how much insurance is going to cost. As long as he is driving, he should be paying you for the addition to your policy, whether he owns a car or not. If he wants to drive, there is a price to pay. It is a privilege, not a right. If you give a car to your son and pay for all of the expenses, it is just a very large toy and he will treat it as such.

At this point, your son is getting to be an interesting person. Listen to him, ask him what he thinks, and include him in family discussions. What you don't want to do is treat him like a friend. He doesn't need a friend, what he needs is a parent. You can certainly be friendly with him, just always remember that you are in charge. Your house, your rules—within reason. He is expected to treat both of his parents with respect, but you should return the favor. He is growing up, and he needs your support to do so successfully.

A boy this age needs parents who appreciate the person he is becoming and who will help him mature into adulthood by providing some structure and guidance. He can look and sound like an adult, but remember, he is not there yet. Don't be shocked when he makes mistakes, but help him work through dealing with the results of his actions.

Becoming a Man

One of these days, you will hear others start referring to your son as a man, and when that happens, you may be surprised. Not to worry, you will probably always think of him as your boy, but you do want to make sure that you provide an environment in which he has the chance to become a man. I'll be frank on this topic: I'm a woman and have no clue what it is like to be a man. What I'm going to tell you now I learned from watching my husband and from discussing this topic with the men at the boys' schools I work with. One of the major issues that boys' schools deal with is helping their students develop into good men.

Here's a true story that will serve to illustrate much of what we know about how boys become men. Some years ago, South Africa had a problem with too many elephants in some of their animal parks and not enough in others. The decision was made to move a bunch of young male elephants from one park to another one where there were no other elephants. Before long it was apparent that the young elephants were terrorizing and killing white rhinos. The elephants had sorted themselves into several groups and were cornering the rhinos, beating them with sticks they picked up with their trunks, and stomping on them. While it is not unusual for elephants to attack rhinos, they customarily only do so when they or their calves are threatened. What made this notable was that the elephants appeared to do it for sport.

The decision was made to bring in some adult male elephants to see if they could serve as good examples of proper elephant behavior. The results were astounding. In short order, the older males let the young males know that their behavior was unacceptable. When the young elephants started to attack the rhinos, the adults would hit them with their trunks to move them away from the rhinos. Additionally, the adult males would threaten the young elephants and force them to back down. Before long, the wild, aggressive youngsters had stopped attacking the rhinos and had started following their elders around, mimicking their behavior.

ROLE MODELS

Without adult males to show them what proper elephant behavior was supposed to be like, the young elephants started acting like gang members. When the adults came on the scene, they had no hesitation in correcting the young ones and making sure that they conformed to proper elephant behavior. What this story tells us is that young boys need to be around adult males to learn what acceptable behavior is for men.

Today, the number of young boys who are raised in a household without any resident adult males is growing by leaps and bounds. Even if adult males are part of the family, they are usually not around very much and sometimes are not seen as decision makers by the children. Boys need to be around good men to become good men. There is some concern that boys raised without access to adult males either use the examples of the women around them as role models or go off on their own and invent their own version of what men should be. Neither will serve boys well in their path to become good men.

One part of his self-concept is the discovery of what sort of a man he will be. Gender identity is the part of our self-understanding that determines whether we think of ourselves as male or female. Do we deal with the world from a masculine or a feminine approach? As adults, we know that this is very complicated and that our understanding of our gender and our sex is linked to much of what we think about ourselves. As we develop our sense of who we are, we tend to think of ourselves in absolutes: I'm good at this skill or I can't do that. Over time, we realize that this isn't true: our skills and abilities can change depending on a host of variables. This is true for our gender identity as well. For example, men talk about their "feminine side" and women work hard to become more assertive, but it takes time for anyone to become comfortable with their identity, gender or otherwise.

Children need to have a wide variety of role models for many reasons, but especially because they need to see that there are many ways to be a man or a woman. Girls usually have lots of role models in their mothers, in their teachers, and in women they meet in many locations. Boys, on the other hand, frequently do not know a lot of men. Many boys do not live with a resident adult male and usually the only men in an elementary school are found in the front office, the gym, or the maintenance department. There is a great deal of concern among those who work with young boys that they are not exposed to enough positive male role models.

Some of the nonacademic men in elementary schools can make a huge difference in boys' lives. I was astounded at one boys' school to find out the custodian was included in faculty meetings because he was someone to whom the boys turned when they were in trouble. His grandson had been a student in the school and the boy introduced his classmates to his grandfather. The boys benefited from talking to an older man who did not have academic control over them.

Make sure that your son has the opportunity to get to know a wide variety of men. Because of their work, resident fathers may not have a lot of time to spend with their sons and they need to make an effort to do so. Even just reading to their sons at night as they go to bed can make a huge difference for a boy. One reason that Boy Scouts is a popular organization is that the program provides adult males who want to give their time to working with boys. If your son is enrolled in an after-school program, make sure that the staff includes males. Frequently, high school students who are required to perform community service can serve as great role models. Your elementary school child will think they are grown-ups even if you know they are not. Grandfathers, uncles, and neighbors can help as well; Dennis the Menace spends more time with Mr. Wilson than he does with his own father.

Divorce or separation

The most likely role model for a boy is his father even if he is no longer in a relationship with the boy's mother. Remember that males may be more emotional than females, and if the relationship between mother and father comes apart, the man may be very hurt. He may show that hurt by withdrawing from the mother and, unfortunately, from his children as well. If the mother is the custodial parent, she needs to make a concerted effort to help her son keep in contact with his father. That can be frustrating, but remember that the distance the man puts between himself and his former family is probably based not in his lack of concern but in his need to protect himself. Not wise, but understandable.

If the relationship between the parents is a serious problem, both parents need to find a neutral person who will help to make sure that all children, but especially the boys, have the opportunity to be with both parents. That person can also monitor the parents' communication, making sure they don't share with the children their hostile feelings about each other. It is no business of the children how crazy one former spouse makes the other; those problems belong only to the adults. How parents treat their children is usually totally different from how they treat each other. Most importantly, one parent should not use access to the children as a weapon to control the other parent. Almost certainly that will result in the noncustodial parent walking away. Boys need both parents, but they particularly need their fathers—especially if they are to become successful fathers themselves one day.

Teachers

When our son was in elementary school, I took great comfort in the statement that as long as a child has one good year out of the first three, he will do all right in school. I'm not sure that is true, but he did have a rocky beginning and turned out fine. Children tend to believe that when things go wrong it is their fault, so many children who have trouble in school assume that they are simply not good students. One boy who had trouble early in school was told by his teacher that he was good in math. He told his mother that the teacher was wrong because he knew he wasn't good at school. His mother tried to point out that he could be good at one part of school and not so good at another. It took this boy several years to understand that concept, and for a long time he prefaced all of his statements about his performance in school with, "Well, you know I'm no good at school . . ."

Your job is to give your son the verbal skills he needs to succeed in school and to acquire some self-management techniques that will make his active nature less of a problem in class. For example, one little boy was suspended from school because he preferred to kneel in his seat as he worked rather than sitting in a conventional manner. The teacher was not able to realize that the kneeling boy was quieter and more focused than the sitting boy and looked at the boy's inability to sit as direct disobedience. The boy did not have the verbal skills to explain all of this to his teacher, however, and when he brought home a disciplinary notice, he was only able to tell his mother "the teacher hates me." If your son can tell you that he prefers to kneel in his chair, then you can help him plan how he can discuss this with the teacher so that it is obvious he is not disobeying, but that he is trying to control himself so he can be quiet and focused in class.

That is the real job of the parent of a boy: mom or dad is not to be his teacher but his helper, seeing that he acquires the skills necessary to interface with his world. You are not required to teach your child to read, write, and calculate. But if you read to your son, you will help him learn to enjoy stories. If you share with your son what you are doing, such as reading the labels on food in the grocery store and the information that you use from those labels, he will discover why he needs to learn to read. If you work with your son to prepare thank-you notes to family and friends and require him to leave notes for you when he has changes in plans, he will learn why writing is important. If you help him learn to count change, make him responsible for his allowance, and keep him on a budget, he will discover the necessity of being conversant with the basics of numbers.

You can help the teacher as well by providing information about what works with your son. Listen to the teacher so that you can help your son understand what is actually being required of him. Sometimes teachers do not always get the point across to all the children in the class because most of the children in the class understood what the teacher said. Remember, school is all about learning to get along with lots of other children in the classroom and being a part of joint learning activities. You can help your son and his teacher by listening to both of them.

You may find it instructive to spend some time in your son's classroom, which may give you insight into how the teacher manages the class. Be careful, however, not to abuse this privilege. Your presence in the classroom can be distracting for all of the students, especially your son. You will find that you are more welcome if you come in for a purpose, such as helping with a class project or preparing food for a special occasion. If your schedule permits, ask the teacher how you can volunteer to help. I taught full-time while my son was in elementary school, but I did help when I could, especially when the class was covering information that was in my teaching area. My husband is self-employed and can make his own schedule, so frequently he was one of the parent chaperones on school trips. Seeing our son in a group setting helped us figure out what he meant when he described his teacher and his classmates.

If you see that your son's needs are not being met in class, ask for a conference with the teacher or invite the teacher to visit you at home. Seeing a child where he is most comfortable can be illuminating for a teacher. Remember that your son is not the only child in the class, so try to see the teacher's point of view. Ask what you can do to help make the difference for your son. If his reading skills are not developing as rapidly as the rest of the class, ask for recommendations of what you can do that will help other than reading to him. I know of one mother who was very concerned about her boy and his lack of reading progress, and the teacher recommended a home program to help. The teacher was dubious that the mother would follow through with the program, but she did and the boy is now a stellar reader. On the other hand, if you know that your son is slow to develop in other areas, don't stress him to the point where he begins to believe that he will never succeed in school.

There may come a time when you have tried everything you can reasonably think of to work with your son's teacher, but your son is still having trouble. Where do you go from here? If the teacher that your son had the year before is still available, ask him or her for suggestions. Ask the present teacher if the previous teacher can be included in a conference. You should have been given a list of administrators to whom you can appeal for help. Start by asking your son's teacher to include the appropriate administrator. What you want to try to do is to continue to include the teacher in your search for help for your son. Excluding the teacher will probably lead to hard feelings, and that won't help anyone. If you continue to have trouble getting help for your son, keep trying. If you don't agree with the answers the school is giving you, it doesn't mean that they are wrong any more than it means that they are right. Sometimes time alone will provide better solutions for academic issues than any treatment or program.

Early identification of problems

Just because your son is a boy does not mean he will have trouble in school, but it is more likely that he will. The issue may not be that he has learning disabilities but that his developmental progress or his learning strengths do not match what the teacher thinks is necessary to be a good student. Yes, teachers should know that children have different approaches to learning, and good teachers do. However, when you are having to manage a lot of children in one room and you are under a great deal of pressure to make sure that the students are successful on a standardized test, it may just be easier to look at those who learn in a more active way as disabled. What you as a parent can do is to help your son develop some skills in adapting his learning strengths to the auditory and verbal approaches preferred by many teachers.

If the school suggests that perhaps your son has learning issues, don't panic. Much of what the school will provide in the way of assistance actually does help and can make a huge difference in the way your son thinks about himself as a student. The major issue is that your son can be labeled as disabled even after he has acquired the skills that were lacking. The help he will receive is important, and if he truly needs the help, make sure that he gets it. Once he is back on track, then you can approach the school to make sure that he is reevaluated.

It is also important that you recognize that your boy may not fit the norm. When I was little, a boy I went to school with was fascinated by dinosaurs. It was not an interest that anyone else shared with him, though, and I learned later that the school was concerned about his having a learning disability because he was so obsessed with dinosaurs. That boy turned into a paleontologist, but when baseball was the prevailing interest for most boys, he was considered strange. Today, dinosaurs would be considered a normal interest for boys. Your boy may just be ahead of the curve! But the school may not agree with you or with him, so you need to be an advocate for your son. The more you understand his strengths and weaknesses and are honest about those to yourself and the school, the better you will be able to help him.

BOYS, PARENTS, AND SCHOOL

Boys are having so much trouble in school today because all children are obliged to go further in education than was customary years ago. A century ago the issue of whether or not a child graduated from high school, much less college, really didn't matter. It was the rare child who completed 16 years of education, and few jobs of any kind required much more than completing the eighth grade. Boys whose learning style did not conform to long-term classroom learning were not in academic difficulty because those boys learned a trade by serving an apprenticeship or taking technical courses. In the 1920s, my father got a bachelor's degree in law in three years right out of high school and passed the bar exam to practice law even though he had not yet received an undergraduate degree from college. Today, you have to complete four years of undergraduate study and three years of law school in order to practice law. A high school diploma is required for almost every job, and some years of post-high school education are required for many jobs that provide a reasonable standard of living.

We, as parents, need to help our sons adapt to the new scholastic requirements without letting them feel as if they are either incompetent or second-class citizens in the world of education. Because of the nature of boys—competitive, physical, group-oriented, active, hands-on—it is hard for parents to help without ending up doing things for them. When you get it right, however, the results are wonderful. You get a confident young man who knows who he is and sort of what he wants. Oh, don't delude yourself into thinking that if you do parenting right your 25-year-old son will be totally sure of what he wants in life. Some do and some don't.

The other factor you need to be aware of is that the boy may be totally sure of what he wants and the man not so much, and that is normal. For example, community colleges are used to dealing with three major groups of students: young women right out of high school who for one reason or another are not able to go to a four-year college; older women who are going back to school after raising a family; and men in their 30s who have finally realized they need more education but are not entirely sure what they are interested in.

All of this takes time—a lot of time—but the benefits are incalculable. You only have one chance with a child, so don't let the time slip through your fingers because you had other obligations. Once you get used to including your child in a lot of what you do, you will realize that even a six-year-old can understand the basics of budgeting and how to balance time and work.

Between 6 and 16, school is the place where your son will spend more of his life than anywhere else—except in bed. Yes, there are people who did poorly in school and who were great successes in life, as well as people who starred in school and have not accomplished much as adults. However, the lessons you learn in school lay the groundwork for everything else that you do. I know I am no good if I try to do something at the last minute; it never works out. I have to talk out a topic to myself in order for me to understand the material. I figured out how I learned over time and then began to realize that my approach worked with many of my boy students.

It is my belief that the various approaches to learning are brain based and environmentally shaped. If these differences were totally due to the way the brain is configured, neither parents nor teachers would have any influence. Yet we know that they do. On the other hand, there are limits to what children and adults can learn to do that are most definitely associated with the brain. Is my inability to remember what I hear due to training—no one made me remember what I heard—or due to some pattern in the way my brain stores information? Is the reason why my son has almost total recall for what he hears due to his compensation for a slow start in reading—he couldn't read what the teacher wrote on the board but could remember it as she said it—or due to some innate ability to remember auditory information that has resulted in his being a good musician? I have no idea, and I know that no one else does either. Both explanations for my son and me are equally valid, and I suspect neither reason totally explains our totally opposite auditory memories.

You can help your son by recognizing his strengths and helping him use those strengths to compensate for his weaknesses. That is a lesson I wish I had learned earlier. We focused so much on our son's shortcomings in reading that we did not notice his strength in auditory memory. Helping him see that while he had trouble in one area he shone in another would have gone a long way toward his feeling more confident in school.

What can parents do to help their sons succeed in school?

What follows is a list of ten steps that will help you provide the framework for your son to do well. I make no guarantees about success in school, but most children can do moderately well as long as they can read, listen, follow directions, and accept that school is important in their lives. At the very least, you *must* do the first.

1. **Read to your son every night.**
   This helps him develop language and listening skills

2. **Turn off the TV and computer** (or at least limit the amount of access).
   This encourages him to develop his imagination and problem solving skills

3. **Talk and sing with your son.**
   This helps your son develop communication skills with others.

4. **Play games with him.**
   This teaches your son to follow rules, problem solve, and lose with dignity.

5. **Let him play by himself or with others without adult interference.**
   This allows him to become self-reliant and deal with others proactively.

6. **Allow him to take risks.**
   This motivates him and allows him think creatively.

7. **Give him chores.**
   This teaches him responsibility and reliability.

8. **Teach him the value of money.**
   This develops a sense of perspective on what is important and the difference between needs and wants.

9. **Teach him to respect others.**
   This allows him to develop self-respect and to be a positive member of his community.

10. **Make no threats, only promises.**
   This gives him structure to his life.

Boys are wonderful creatures. What you see is exactly what is there; rarely do they have hidden agendas. If they like you, boys will tell you, and if they don't like you, they won't cover it up. Remember, boys will be boys longer than girls will be girls, so don't expect your boy to keep up with the girls of his age, especially as they go through puberty. Enjoy your boy. He will grow up soon enough and you will miss the silly jokes and the flying hugs. Help him respect himself and find out what he is all about. That is what he needs from you.

RESOURCES AND HELPS

———

I sincerely hope this book has provided you with a deeper understanding of your boy as he grows up, but I realize it cannot possibly have answered all of the questions surrounding your son's development. For interested parents, here is a list of books, video games, Internet sources, schools, and other resources you may find helpful.

Books for Parents

While this book is designed for parents, it does not cover every topic in detail. Following are some books that you may find interesting. This list does not pretend to give you every book that has been published about boys, but I have included some current ones that are solidly based on science and are written by people who work closely with boys. The list is shorter rather than longer on the theory that too many books may be overwhelming. Some of these books are not exclusively about boys, but nonetheless provide good insights into problems inherent with boys.

- Allen, J., & Allen, C. W. (2009). *Escaping the Endless Adolescence: How We Can Help Our Teenagers Grow Up Before They Grow Old.* New York, NY: Ballentine Books.
- Cox, A. J. (2005). *Boys of Few Words: Raising Our Sons to Communicate and Connect.* New York, NY: The Guilford Press.
- Rao, A., & Seaton, M. (2009). *The Way of Boys: Raising Healthy Boys in a Challenging and Complex World.* New York, NY: William Morrow.
- Sax, L. (2007). *Boys Adrift: The Five Factors Driving the Growing Epidemic of Unmotivated Boys and Underachieving Young Men.* New York, NY: Basic Books.
- Thompson, M., & Barker, T. (2000). *Speaking of Boys: Answers to the Most-Asked Questions About Raising Sons.* New York, NY: Ballentine Books.
- Thompson, M., O'Neill-Grace, C., & Cohen, L. J. (2002). *Best Friends, Worst Enemies: Understanding the Social Lives of Children.* New York, NY: Ballentine Books.
- Tyre, P. (2008). *The Trouble With Boys: A Surprising Report Card on Our Sons, Their Problems at School, and What Parents and Educators Must Do.* New York, NY: Crown Publishers.

Some of you will want sources that are more scientific or that go into a bit more depth. The authors of the following books are all neuroscientists who have written texts that are accessible to those of you who are interested in accessing the science cited in the text. You will find a wide variety of opinions in these books so if you do read them, don't be surprised if you end by being somewhat confused—we all are to one extent or another.

- Baron-Cohen, S. (2003). *The Essential Difference: The Truth About the Male and Female Brain.* New York, NY: Basic Books.
- Eliot, L. (2009). *Pink Brain, Blue Brain: How Small Differences Grow Into Troublesome Gaps—and What We Can Do About It.* Boston, MA: Houghton Mifflin Harcourt.
- Fine, C. (2010). *Delusions of Gender: The Real Science Behind Sex Differences.* New York, NY: W. W. Norton & Company, Inc.
- Hines, M. (2004). *Brain Gender.* New York, NY: Oxford University Press.
- Maccoby, E. E. (1998). *The Two Sexes: Growing up Apart, Growing Together.* Cambridge, MA: Harvard University Press.

One of the problems with raising boys is the fact that boys need physical and dangerous play. These books will help you get in touch with your "inner boy." Remember that if it isn't dangerous or challenging, boys won't think it is worth doing.

- Conner, B. (2007). *Unplugged Play: No Batteries. No Plugs. Pure Fun.* New York, NY: Workman Publishing Company.
- Davis, T. (2010). *Handy Dad: 25 Awesome Projects for Dads and Kids.* San Francisco, CA: Chronicle Books.
- DeBenedet, A. T., & Cohen, L. J. (2010). *The Art of Roughhousing: Good Old-Fashioned Horseplay and Why Every Kid Needs It.* Philadelphia, PA: Quirk Books.
- Gurstell, W. (2001). *Backyard Ballistics: Build Potato Cannons, Paper Match Rockets, Cincinnati Fire Kites, Tennis Ball Mortars, and More Dynamite Devices.* Chicago, IL: Chicago Review Press.
- Iggulden, C., & Iggulden, H. (2007). *The Dangerous Book for Boys.* New York, NY: William Morrow.

Books for Boys

This is a list of classics and some books you may not have thought of for your son. Don't forget that facile readers may be able to read books whose subject matter is a bit beyond them. The Harry Potter series is a perfect example. The first book in the series is rated for fifth or sixth grade, partially because of the complexity of the language, but also because of the topics. The later books are definitely for older children. Younger children may be able to read the books, but may be disturbed or fail to understand what is going on. After all, people die in the Potter books, which is a topic children need to face, but you will want to be careful. Be sure that your child is ready to deal with the situations that arise in the story. I suggest that you read the book *with* your child and be prepared to answer his questions frankly and openly. While reading the last part of *The Once and Future King* by T. H. White, my son asked me why Arthur was so upset with his wife Guinevere and his best friend Lancelot. This led to us having a discussion about marital infidelity which was not a topic that I thought a 12 year-old would have been interested in. But this allowed me to let him know what his parents thought about that topic in a non-personal way, giving him information he could use in the future.

Kathleen Odean's *Great Books for Boys* (Ballantine Books, 1998) is simply a list of books that may help you find something for you to read to your son or for him to read on his own.

The following is a list of authors whose books appeal to most boys. Some of these are for younger boys such as Scarry and Sendak and some are for adolescents such as Adams and Card. Others are books written for adults that adolescents have found interesting such as Hemingway and Hillerman. However, a young reader with good skills may want to attempt books that are written for older boys and an older reader whose skills are still developing may feel more comfortable with books written at a simpler reading level. Some of the authors have written books for adults as well as for young adults. In general, their adult books will be suitable for adolescents but not for middle school children. These authors' names will be followed by "YA" so that you will know to be careful when selecting books for your younger child. All other authors do not write for both groups. If you are not sure what age group the author's books will appeal to, check with a librarian or your son's teacher. I've divided this list into two groups, younger and older, only because some parents might not be familiar with some of the authors. Younger is elementary school and older is middle and high school.

YOUNGER BOYS

Boys will enjoy most books for children of this age as long as they are funny or silly and don't involve perfect children. Boys in this age group like stories about silly monsters, about animals and dragons, about trucks and trains, about superheroes, about how the real world works, about gross bodily functions (*Walter the Farting Dog* springs to mind), and about children who are loud and active—just like them. They almost never like books that people think children should like or stories that teach a moral.

Look for books by: Jeff Brown, Jeff Kinney, Bill Peet, Dav Pilkey, Jack Prelutsky, Richard Scarry, Maurice Sendak, Dr. Seuss, Jon Scieszka, William Steig, Mo Willems.

OLDER BOYS

If your son is reading for pleasure by the time he gets to middle school, you have prepared him well. Your task now will be to keep him reading as there will be lots of pressure for him to shift over to computer and TV entertainment. Boys of this age will read almost any type of book except for those plainly written for girls such as romance novels. However, you will find that your son is likely fascinated by one genre or another and will read everything in that category to the exclusion of other types of books. Do what you can to expand his horizons. Some of these authors write books for adults as well, so if the name is followed by "YA" check to make sure that the selection is appropriate for your young adult reader.

Books by: Douglas Adams, Lloyd Alexander, Ray Bradbury, Kristen Britain, Orson Scott Card (YA), Tom Clancy, Eoin Colfer, Susan Cooper, Cressida Cowell, Stephen Crane, Roald Dahl (YA), Arthur Conan Doyle, Alexandre Dumas, Paul Gallico, Neil Gaiman (YA), Jack Gantos, The Brothers Grimm, Frank Herbert, Carl Hiaasen (YA), Ernest Hemingway, Tony Hillerman, Brian Jacques, Diana Wynne Jones, Stephen King, Rudyard Kipling, Jon Krakauer, Madeline L'Engle, Jack London, George R. R. Martin, Anne McCaffery, L. E. Modesitt Jr., Garth Nix, Christopher Paolini, Gary Paulsen, Daniel Pinkwater, Phillip Pullman, Terry Pratchett, Rick Riordan, J. K. Rowling, Salman Rushdie (YA), Louis Sachar, Lemony Snicket, John Steinbeck, R. L. Stine, J.R.R. Tolkien, Mark Twain,

Jules Verne, Kurt Vonnegut, E. B. White, Tad Williams (YA), Jane Yolen, and Paul Zindel.

There are also many nonfiction books that appeal to boys. These books can become among your son's favorite reads and you may be mystified because they seem to be composed of pictures or lists.

Aronson, M., & Newquist, H. P. (2007). *For Boys Only. The Biggest, Baddest Book Ever.* New York, NY: Feiwel & Friends Publishing.

Campbell, G. (2009). *The Boys' Book of Survival (How to Survive Anything, Anywhere).* New York, NY: Scholastic Nonfiction.

DK series. New York, NY: DK Publishing. This is a U.K. series of science and animals that boys really warm up to. The pictures are wonderful and there are a huge number of topics. Any bookstore will be happy to help you find titles by this group and you can also find them in Internet bookstores by looking up DK Publishing.

Dunham, K., & Bjorkman, S. (2007). *The Boys' Body Book: Everything You Need To Know For Growing Up YOU.* New York, NY: Applesauce Press.

Guiness Book of World Records. (latest). New York, NY: Bantam Books.

GRAPHIC NOVELS

Some graphic novels are basically comic books, but the best of them do have a plot, characters, and involve following a story line. Be careful when selecting these as some are rewritten and others are abridged. You do not want the rewritten ones. The first ones listed below are abridged versions of classic works. Search for these in your favorite online bookstore by the first general term and then find the specific book. The point is to get boys to read and if they will look at these, then they will begin to read them.

Puffin Graphics: *Call of the Wild* by London, *Treasure Island* by Stevenson, *Black Beauty* by Brigman, *Red Badge of Courage* by Crane, *Frankenstein* by Shelly, *The Wizard of Oz* by Baum, *Dracula* by Stoker, and *Macbeth* by Shakespeare.

Graphic Classics: these are all collections of short stories either by one author or with a common theme. Arthur Conon Doyle, E. A. Lovecraft, Edgar Allen Poe, *Edgar Allen Poe's Tales of Mystery*, Robert Louis Stevenson, Bram Stoker, Mark Twain, H. G. Wells, Western Classics, African-American Classics, Fantasy Classics, Christmas Classics, Horror Classics, Science Fiction Classics, Adventure Classics, Gothic Classics.

Classical Comics: these are from England, and the Shake-speare plays all come in two versions, one in the traditional Elizabethan English and one in modern English. *Macbeth*, *Romeo and Juliet*, *A Midsummer Night's Dream*, *The Tempest*, *Henry V*, *Wuthering Heights*, *Dracula*, *Great Expectations*, *The Canterville Ghost*, *Jane Eyre*, and *A Christmas Carol*. By the time you look for these, there will very likely be more.

Series of books that have been turned into graphic versions, probably because they appeal to boys, are: *Redwall* by Jacques, *The Boxcar Children* by Warner, *Artemis Fowl* by Colfer.

Some books were graphic to begin with: *The Adventures of Tintin* by Hergé (be careful here, all other versions are tie-ins to the recent movie; this was originally written in French, so make sure that you get a translated version by Hergé that your son can read. Also, there are many books in the series by the original author), *The Alex Rider* series by Horowitz and Johnston, and many of Neil Gaiman's books.

There are now available lots of movie tie-in books to superhero movies, science fiction movies, and the whole vampire craze. I leave that to your discretion as to whether or not you want your son reading that sort of material, remembering that if he is reading anything, he *is* reading. Fluency comes from repetition and if he will read, even if you are not thrilled with the genre, he is processing words.

Manga is the term for comics created either in Japan or in a style similar to Japanese books – that means that the book opens left to right, not right to left as is common for books written for alphabetic languages. For a child who is having trouble learning to read, getting used to the backwards orientation is probably not going to help him. Additionally, much of the subject matter is either violent, sexist or both. There are some titles which are acceptable for younger children up to age 16. The books about Astro Boy are good for boys, but your son will probably not be interested in those about Sailor Moon and her Sailor friends. The web site www.comicsworthreading.com is list of informal reviews of manga and other graphic materials and provides some ratings about which titles are appropriate for younger children. This site has a very long list of various graphic materials.

Video Games

Action games (which includes the shooter games), adventure games, racing games, role playing (can be live action role playing), simulation games, and strategy games are, at the moment, the major categories of video games. No list I could provide would keep up with the latest game that your son wants to play, but you want to make sure that your son does not get addicted to a particular type of game. It is not that video games are bad, the problem involves playing such games to the exclusion of any other activity, particularly when a child plays the same type of game all the time. Encourage your son to play games that are as interactive as possible such as the physically interactive games now available. What you want to discourage is your son, by himself for hours, playing a first-person shooter game.

The Entertainment Software Rating Board is responsible for deciding for which age group a game is appropriate. Their web site is www.esrb.org. There are also quite a lot of web sites that review video games. The folks at C-Net have a good reputation for fairness so you might start with www.cnet.com/games/. New Egg is a great web site for computer-related information and the people who buy from them usually are very accurate with their reviews. Not all games are rated, but when they are, the rating is useful. The web address is www.newegg.com and you will see the gaming button on the left hand side of the home page.

Internet Sources

If you look up "programs for boys" on the Internet, you will be overwhelmed with the variety of choices available. Many provide mentors for boys who are missing strong parental models or teachers for boys whose learning issues mean that school is not comfortable. Be careful in choosing such programs, as not all are as helpful as they claim to be. If you decide that such a program looks good for your son, ask to speak to other parents whose children have been in the program. If possible, visit the site before you sign your son up.

Schools for Boys

There are many educational programs for boys both in single gender schools and in coed schools. The growing number of single gender classes in the public school system is testament to the effectiveness of such programs. No program is perfect and your son may not benefit from such a school, but these programs have helped many children.

NASSPE: The National Association for Single-Sex Public Education is the organization that provides information and training for schools with single gender programs primarily in the United States, but also schools in other countries. Many of the member schools are coed schools with single gender classes for some students. Check out their website: http://www.singlesexschools.org/

COSEBOC: Coalition of Schools Educating Boys of Color is a group of primarily public and charter schools in the United States whose student body includes African-American,

Hispanic, Latino, Native American, Polynesian, and Asian students. You'll find them at: www.coseboc.org

IBSC: The International Boys' Schools Coalition is a group of boys' schools around the world who promote the education of boys. In the United States, most of the members are private schools, but not all. Many of the international members are state schools. Their website is: www.theibsc.org

NAIS: The National Association of Independent Schools is the organization for private schools in the United States. Many of their member schools are either boys' schools or have programs for boys' education. Check them out at: www.nais.org

TABS: The Association of Boarding Schools is a group of residential schools, some of which are single gender. Most of these schools are very aware of the needs of boys in education and can provide a great education if your son needs a new environment. You'll find them at: www.boarding-schools.com

After-school: One concern is what to do with boys after school and before parents return home from work. Sports works well in high school, but not all boys are interested in sports or in a variety of sports which will keep them busy all year long. Look for programs such as the Boys and Girls Club at www.bgca.org, after school programs run by your school system or by your local YMCA or YWCA, after-school robotics programs, your local parks and recreation department, 4-H clubs, Odyssey of the Mind, and Destination ImagiNation. What you want is something for your son that encourages him to move, engage with his world, and think, but not in a way that is like what he has been doing in school. Most importantly, your boy needs to move after school, not simply watch TV or play video games.

Educational Consultants

If you believe that your son needs to make a change, an educational consultant can provide a lot of information. Families often consult these experts as part of the college/career choice process, but if you believe that your child needs another educational program, an educational consultant can help you find alternative programs. Please be careful, educational consultants are just as likely to see boys as problems in the classroom as are teachers, probably because many of them were teachers. As with finding help in any area, ask around for recommendations. Especially pay attention to how the individual sees boys in school.

Many consultants are qualified to perform educational testing, and if not, will know of those in your area who are so qualified. The assumption should not be that the boy has learning issues, but that testing will reveal a boy's learning strengths so that the consultant can help you come to a mutually agreed solution to your son's academic difficulties. If the individual seems to be sure that learning differences will be found, find another consultant.

You will find that educational testing can be very pricy and as with all things, you get what you pay for. If your son is in a public school, testing is provided through the school, but you may have to wait for him to get an appointment. If you are near a college or university with a school of education, you may find that students do testing under supervision. That can be a very viable solution, especially since the student is likely to be aware of up-to-date testing instruments and educational solutions.

The website for the Independent Educational Consultants Association will provide a great deal of information about their services as well as help you find a certified consultant. Find them at: www.educationalconsulting.org. A similar organization is the American Institute of Certified Educational Planners. Find them at: www.aicep.org

Gap Year Sources

The point of a gap year, or even two, is for a boy to have some time away from the academic grind, but still be in a structured environment. The boy should have an experience that engages his interests and exposes him to new situations perhaps in a place far away from home. This program is well known in Europe and you will find many young people from England and France working for a year in the U.S. before returning to school.

There are a growing number of programs in the United States, many of them sponsored by well-known colleges and universities. You can simply search on "gap year" on the Internet and you will be surprised by all of the possibilities. Here are some sites that may provide interesting and fruitful alternatives to going straight to college:

> www.planetgapyear.com
>
> www.letsgetglobal.org
>
> www.gapyear365.com
>
> www.interimprograms.com
>
> www.gapyear.com
>
> www.gap-year.com
>
> www.realgap.com

There are some other possibilities for a boy to take a break from school. Such programs include the following outdoors programs:

> www.nols.ed
>
> www.outwardbound.org

The advantage of these programs is that the participant has the chance to test himself in a real situation. Some of these programs are designed as survival training and for the boy who has never had the chance to interact with nature, these can be life changing.

If you have further questions:

This book is aimed for most problems that most parents will deal with. Nonetheless, there will be questions which I have not answered. If you have questions, feel free to contact me via: http://abigailnorfleetjames.com/contact/ but know that I reserve the right to put your question and my answer on my blog—if you look at the questions that are answered there, you will see that the questioner is not identified in any way.

Your son is lucky—you cared enough to ask the right questions.

APPENDIX

WEAPONS OF MASS DESTRUCTION

I went to college in the Age of Aquarius. Consequently, despite the fact that I was raised in the country (and was used to seeing guns as a child), I was determined that my son would never have a gun to play with. When he was four years old, I found him in the backyard whittling away on a piece of wood with a very sharp stone. "What are you doing?" I asked. "Making a pistol." I have no idea how he even knew what a pistol was. He was never allowed to watch anything other than PBS children's shows, and his only playmate was a girl whose favorite toy at the time was a play kitchen. We had a rifle in the house, which I know he had never seen because it was at the top of a very tall closet behind pillows and he could not have reached the rifle without knocking the pillows down.

I was horrified. Then I realized that like it or not, he was interested in guns, and friends whose own sons had expressed fascination with guns assured me that keeping them from him wasn't going to reduce his interest. What concerned me was that most of the guns I had played with as a girl were cap pistols, and we could point them at each other with impunity. Those are no longer available because of the noise made by the exploding caps, but what I disliked about cap pistols was that you could point the gun at someone and basically nothing happened. I wanted my son to know that there were consequences to guns, so my husband and I got him several of the devices that fired foam missiles and balls. He soon discovered they were not totally benign because they did knock over small lamps and, once, a porcelain dish, so he learned that they were outside toys.

Boys are attracted to objects that seem very dangerous to parents, but the solution is not to keep them away from boys. The solution is to give them to boys *in a safer form*, such as the foam guns. If they are too safe, your son won't be interested. Yes, he runs the risk of cutting himself or breaking a window, but that is how he is going to learn to be cautious and to protect himself from harm. Keeping him from these objects only makes them more attractive. Some boys will not be interested in these objects, so don't press them on your son, but do offer to supply these risky objects. By the way, if your son breaks a window, he pays for the repair, and if he is old enough, he learns to replace it himself.

The most important point is that at the beginning, you need to be present when your son uses these objects, but when you see that he knows how to manage them, you should give him some space in which to work with them on his own. I know that they are all dangerous, but you don't want to keep your son away from these because if he shows an interest, he will sneak ways to get and play with them. What you want is for your son to learn to *use them safely*. Then your job is to trust him to use them correctly.

Of course this isn't a complete list. Sorry, but boys have been coming up with variations on these themes since someone first picked up a rock. However, I have yet to run into a boy who is interested in all of these, so take heart that once your son finds his risky pleasure, he is likely to stick with it. And, if you are lucky, he will be happy to shoot basketballs instead of targets.

Scissors

You should make sure that your son has a pair of his own scissors by the time he is four or five and that the left-handed child gets a pair that work for him. These should not be the plastic ones that really won't cut; give him an actual pair of metal ones with rounded tips. Then give him magazines and glue and let him have at it, cutting out favorite pictures and making posters or collages.

Don't tell him all the things he isn't allowed to cut up—hair is the usual one. This will only make those objects more attractive. If the unthinkable should occur, don't worry; hair grows back. But get a picture of him or his little sister with the unfortunate cut to show at his rehearsal dinner in about 25 years!

The reason for giving a young boy scissors is that using them teaches him how to coordinate with his hand to accomplish a task. If you don't give him his own scissors, he will find yours, which have sharp points and are very dangerous. Yes, some boys will discover that you can use the edge of one side of the scissors to scrape and that can cause unintended damage. Just remember, no matter what type of boy you have—rambunctious or reserved—by the time he is 16, your house will show evidence of his presence.

Knives

Seventy-five years ago, every boy had a small pocketknife by the time he was 10. Today, we go ballistic if a child brings a butter knife to school to spread cheese on a cracker. Boys need knives, real ones, and they need to know how to use them safely. The knife shouldn't be razor sharp, but my husband says that if the knife is too dull, it can be just as dangerous as if it is too sharp because the boy will push too hard with it. Your son should know that if he uses the knife inappropriately, he will lose it, and it absolutely does not go with him to school. As he gets better with the knife, teach him how to sharpen it and keep it in good shape. If you don't know how, find someone who does.

Let him practice cutting things in the kitchen. He can be responsible for cutting up vegetables on a cutting board once he is eight or so. It's easier to learn how to cut by practicing on softer rather than harder substances, with the advantage that he is also learning the basics of cooking. And by letting him use kitchen knives, you may reduce his drive to get a pocketknife.

Real Tools

Toy manufacturers know that boys love hammers, drills, and saws, and lots of these fundamental tools are available in plastic reproductions, which are totally safe. But your son probably hankers after the real thing. If he does not have anyone in his family who is interested in tools, perhaps a neighbor will allow your son the chance to observe him working and give your son the opportunity to work with some of his tools. You can go to your local hardware store and get your son a small hammer, a hand drill, and a small, not very sharp saw. Combine that with scrap lumber and some nails and he will be happy for a long time. Generally, boys are ready for this around age 10.

If your son expresses an interest in building, do what you can to find him someone who will let him at least watch the process. Anytime a house is being built or repaired, you can usually find all the small boys in the neighborhood just looking on. Scouts and 4-H offer programs in which children learn some basic home repair. Do let your son express this interest if for no other reason than you will now have a handyman around!

Guns and Swords

When I was a girl, every boy had a BB gun, and I was taught to shoot a rifle in summer camp. Children in rural areas have space in which to practice, but children who live in urban or suburban areas do not. The foam substitute will work for a while before your son will start asking for laser tag equipment or, in middle school, to be taken to play paint ball. Summer play is made more fun with water guns but be careful; some are very powerful. As I mentioned earlier, keeping your son from guns will only make them more attractive. If he has the chance to shoot objects he will realize one of two things: either that this sport doesn't interest him or that he really likes to shoot things. If the latter, letting him have access to gunlike toys will mean that he may not be driven to get the real thing. Teaching him responsibility is much better than refusing to let him try a gun. He sees them in all sorts of movies and video games and he wants to try to shoot.

The important lesson is gun safety, so if your son is interested in games that involve guns, such as paint ball, he should take a course in the safe handling of the weapons. Your local supplier of that equipment should be able to supply the name of individuals who offer those courses.

Swords are a different matter, because boys will make them out of whatever is to hand, be it swimming pool noodles or sticks. You don't need to supply these objects, but boys who are involved in hero play will want some equipment. The ones that are made out of hard rubber rather than the cheaper ones made from rigid plastic are probably a bit safer. The *Harry Potter* movies have led to a renaissance in fencing, and you may be able to find lessons in that sport in your area.

Archery is also becoming more popular because of the book and movie based on *The Hunger Games*. The very cheap sets available in toy stores really won't work very well and may be somewhat dangerous because they break unexpectedly. Also, without some training, children using toy sets have little ability to aim the arrows where they want them to go, which can be very dangerous. Competent instruction will provide your son with a chance to use good equipment to see if he is really interested in this sport.

Safety vs. Risk

Most boys, but not all, want to be involved in risky activities. It is quite understandable that you want to keep your son safe, but if you keep him from being involved in risky activities, he will simply do them behind your back. In that case, he won't be using safe equipment and he won't have been taught either the proper handling or the risks involved, so he is more likely to get hurt. What you want is to make these activities less attractive by letting your son learn how to use them. Don't hover too long: he needs the chance to make mistakes and learn from them.

Fireworks and Rockets

There is nothing more fun than shooting objects out of a potato gun made from tennis ball cans. You will find the directions in several of the books listed in the resources, along with other devices designed to propel objects rapidly through space. Learning to put these together using scrap lumber and generous amounts of duct tape will teach your son to be resourceful and independent. Why would he want to do this? I don't know, but he does.

How about fireworks? This depends on your locality, but the small devices usually available around the Fourth of July in most places are pretty safe. They are not entirely safe, however, which is, of course, the attraction. Our son and his father would start planning for the festivities several weeks in advance, clearing a place in our driveway that would provide enough space so that sparks would not set the surroundings on fire, and visiting various booths to find the best bang for their buck. Today, our son continues to do this for his friends, and he has never injured himself, others, or his neighborhood. My husband was wise about escalating the size of the fireworks as our son grew up so it was always exciting.

Rockets that are water or air powered are available for children around eight and up. These are simple to operate and moderately safe. Be careful to look at the suggested ages for these rockets as some are a bit more powerful and are suggested for children ten and up. These may satisfy your son's need to shoot objects straight up in the air. If they don't, the next step, which involves fuel, is for older boys, and I would recommend that you find him a rocketry club where he can be instructed in the art of sending missiles very far in the air. Also, get the movie *October Sky* and watch it with him. Or better yet, give him the book on which the movie was based, *Rocket Boys*. There are also two sequels to the book if he gets fascinated by this real story of how a boy from West Virginia became a rocket scientist.

Flinging Toys

Included in this category of toys are slingshots, darts, boomerangs, rubber band guns, and the like. They are all pretty dangerous mainly because it is really hard to aim with them. On the other hand, for the boy with good hand-eye coordination, they can provide lots of fun. If your son has to have one, provide the smallest you can find and tell him he is only allowed to fling objects at a target outside. Frisbees are the safest in this category and there are many different varieties. Establish a Frisbee golf course in your neighborhood if this seems to be an activity that your son and his crowd are interested in.

Wheels

While objects with wheels may not seem like weapons of mass destruction, if not used properly, they can easily become a problem. Research indicates that boys are very attracted to anything with wheels so you can almost guarantee that your son will want to have one of these.

Tricycles, scooters, bicycles, skates, and skateboards are the basics. There are a great many safety regulations about these, but unfortunately boys don't find the safe use of wheeled toys to be very interesting. Wait until you come home some afternoon to find that your son has constructed a ramp for his tricycle so that he can jump over the sidewalk! At the very least, children should always wear helmets when riding any wheeled toy. Be alert to the fit of the helmet because your child's head will grow a bit. It is very important that the helmet fit properly, and it's worthwhile asking an expert for help with the fit. If your son is reluctant to wear a helmet, try using a superhero theme for decoration. Which brings up a critical topic for you to be aware of: be careful about letting your son ride on his wheeled toy dressed in superhero garb. Capes, in particular, can catch in wheels or other mechanisms and may pull him off of the toy.

As your son grows up, he will graduate to the versions of these toys that have only two wheels and require balance. One day you may find your son racing his bicycle down the sidewalk without the training wheels touching the sidewalk, in which case it is obvious that he is ready to have the trainers removed. Others will take much longer to acquire that skill and will be reluctant to lose the extra wheels. The same will be true of skates. Some children will stay with the traditional four-wheeled versions for a long time even after others will be ready for in-line skates.

Skateboards are the standard in areas where bicycles are too big, such as in cities and more urban areas. Your son will see older boys in his neighborhood with them and ask for one—probably before you are comfortable with his having one. The real issue is that skateboards give children mobility, and the child with a skateboard can go out of his neighborhood very rapidly. You should discuss with your son some guidelines for proper use of the board when you see that he has some skill on it. Make sure, of course, that he has appropriate head, knee, and wrist protection when he rides. Fortunately, wearing the protective gear is considered cool since the professionals wear it. Part of safety is learning that the street is not an appropriate place for a skateboard. Your son will complain that there is no place to skate, so see if you can help him find a surface that can be easily blocked off from cars so that the boys can have a safe place to play.

One of the major problems with boys and skateboards is your neighbors, who may be annoyed by the constant scraping sounds. Think of it like the basketball on the backboard: the sound may be annoying, but you know where he is. Another factor about skateboards is that you rarely find a boy riding alone; skateboarders usually ride in small groups, so that can be an issue for you as well. Who are these children he has met on the street? If your area has a skateboard park, that is a great place for your son to learn the basics and meet other boys interested in riding. On the other hand, some of the apparatus in a park will probably be beyond his ability for a while, although he may not believe that. But that is typical for all toys.

Then there are wheels with motors. Some boys will want to go faster than they can propel themselves and that will require a motor. The first level is small cars with batteries to be used in the backyard. These are not as benign as they look. Check on the Internet for videos of children riding these in unsafe (but amusing) ways. The big issue is that these children are not old enough to appreciate the danger of the road, and they are too small to be seen easily by drivers in big cars. Remember that small children have no concept of braking and don't realize that they need to start to break before they actually want to stop. These toys should only be used with good supervision.

The next level is go-karts. If there is a park near you and your son is interested, take him and some friends for an afternoon. Some boys will find this the most fun they have ever had and others will not be so enthusiastic. Racing go-karts is popular in some areas. If your son wants to get involved with that you should know that it can be very expensive. Also, find someone whose son is already involved and ask lots of questions. Even with roll cages over the top, children do get injured in accidents in this sport.

By the time your son is old enough for his driver's license, he should be well familiar with the rules of the road and your expectations for his behavior in a vehicle. That is one of the reasons for giving him the nonmotorized vehicles, to give him some practice in steering and in finding out the limitations of wheeled vehicles. Motorcycles are popular in my area, but most parents are very careful about letting teens drive or ride them. There is a reason that the medical profession calls motorcycles "organ donors." Even with helmets, protective gear, and other safety equipment, riding motorcycles is dangerous, which is exactly why boys want to. Be careful with the mini-motorcycles. They can be just as dangerous, partially because they don't look like they would be.

Climbing

This doesn't involve dangerous toys, but some boys simply love to climb. Read some of the books by Jon Krakauer to get a glimpse of what drives climbers. One of the Olympic gymnasts was a climber as a little child so his parents gave him gymnastic lessons. If that doesn't satisfy your son, take him to a climbing center and let him try. If he likes it, you will find that he will need to keep climbing higher and higher, but better that he does it safely with training than just flinging himself at a precipice.

Your child is a boy: no matter how much you want to protect him, he wants to engage in risky behavior. Give him the chance when he is little and you will find that he may be more willing to be careful when he is older. It is my observation that the boy who was prevented from dangerous activities when he was little is most likely to do seriously dangerous things when he is older.

ABOUT THE AUTHOR

Prior to obtaining her doctorate from the University of Virginia's Curry School of Education, Abigail Norfleet James taught general science, biology, and psychology in both boys' and girls' secondary schools for many years. Her area of expertise is developmental and educational psychology as applied to the gendered classroom, a subject she now consults with school systems, colleges, and universities on. She is presently an adjunct instructor in education at the University of Virginia's Northern Virginia Center and is an adjunct professor of psychology at Germanna Community College.

Dr. James's publications include reports of research comparing the educational attitudes of male graduates of coed schools to male graduates of single sex schools and research describing the effects of gendered basic skills instruction. In addition, she has written on differentiated instruction at the elementary school level and two books applying cognitive neuropsychology to the classroom: *Teaching the Male Brain: How Boys Think, Feel, and Learn in School*, and *Teaching the Female Brain: How Girls Learn Math and Science*. She is the coauthor of a workbook of interactive lessons titled *Active Lessons for Active Brains: Teaching Boys and Other Experiential Learners, Grades 3–10*. She has presented workshops and papers at many educational conferences around the world and works with teachers and parent groups in interpreting the world of gendered education particularly in the coed classroom. While she writes primarily on the teaching of boys, her work with schools involves teaching both girls and boys.

Her professional affiliations include the American Educational Research Association, the American Psychological Association, the Association for Supervision and Curriculum Development, the Coalition of Schools Educating Boys of Color, the Gender and Education Association, the International Boys' School Coalition, and the National Association for Single Sex Public Education (advisory board member).

CPSIA information can be obtained at www.ICGtesting.com
Printed in the USA
LVOW072139200613

339620LV00002B/59/P